CONTENTS

Chapter 1   Paradigm Shift   5

Natural Disasters

Chapter 2   God's Weapons   14
Chapter 3   The Coming Judgments of God   23
Chapter 4   Signs in the Heavens: Part 1   40
Chapter 5   Signs in the Heavens: Part 2   47
Chapter 6   Balls of Fire   61
Chapter 7   Paradigm Shifts and Bible Prophecy   72
Chapter 8   Paradigm Shifts and Disasters   80

Millennarian Movements

Chapter 9   Disasters and Millennarian Movements   84
Chapter 10   A Modern Deception   92
Chapter 11   A Different View of the End Time   108
Chapter 12   Disasters and the Crisis in Revelation 13   123
Chapter 13   Our Responsibility to the World   134
Chapter 14   Preparing for the Disasters Ahead   140
Chapter 15   Facing the End Time Without Fear   154

Appendix A   Reflections on the Close of Probation   167
Appendix B   Questions About *Christ's Object Lessons*, 412 179

THE COMING GREAT CALAMITY

MARVIN MOORE

Pacific Press Publishing Association
Boise, Idaho
Oshawa, Ontarlo, Canada

Edited by Kenneth R. Wade
Cover art and design by Dennis Ferree

Copyright © 1997 by
Pacific Press Publishing Association
Printed in the United States of America
All Rights Reserved

Moore, Marvin, 1937-
    The coming great calamity / Marvin Moore.
        p.   cm.
    Includes bibliographical references.
    ISBN 0-8163-1354-7 (pbk. : alk. paper)
    1. Bible—Prophecies—End of the world. 2. Seventh-
day Adventists—Doctrines.   I. Title.
BS649.E63M66   1996
236'.9—dc20   96-22749
                                                   CIP

97 98 99 00 01 • 5 4 3 2

CHAPTER ONE

PARADIGM SHIFT

In the fall of 1994, I spent a weekend in the home of a friend in southern California. On Sunday morning, shortly before the time came for me to leave for my plane, I happened to walk through his living room, and on the coffee table I spied a copy of the October issue of *Omni*. I picked up the magazine and started leafing through it, and an article about miraculous appearances of the Virgin Mary caught my attention. Here are a couple of paragraphs from that article:

On March 21, 1994, New York's eleven o'clock Eyewitness News ended with this pious tableau: A solemn, modestly dressed Egyptian immigrant family and their friends crowd an apartment in Bensonhurst, Brooklyn, all of them staring reverently at a glistening copper icon of the Virgin Mary. With detached amusement, the TV anchor announces that this icon, which the Boutros family bought in a church gift shop in Cairo, is weeping oil tears. The camera cuts to an exotic, bearded figure in a long, black cassock, identified as a bishop of the Coptic Orthodox Church, a sect of Christianity hailing from Egypt. He assures the greater New York audience that a miracle has indeed occurred.

Back in the newsroom, the TV anchor smiles in a *who knows* kind of way. The story was clearly meant to be a footnote on the richness of life in the Big City (*Omni*, October 1994, 54).

If you're like the average westerner, you probably heaved a sigh, shook your head, and perhaps joined New York's TV anchor in smiling at how very gullible some people can be. That's my reaction to stories like this, I can assure you.

We need to be careful not to smile too broadly or sigh too loudly, though, because the joke just may be on us.

I don't mean that I think the copper virgin might really have shed miraculous oily tears. If you and I could open up the icon's head, we'd probably find a container of very ordinary cooking oil inside that was connected with a tube to its eyes. And with our rational minds, so carefully honed to look for logical, scientific proof of everything, we'd proclaim the icon a fraud and go on about our business.

The reason the joke might be on us is that more is going on in this story than is apparent to the casual observer, especially those looking at it through Western, scientific eyes. The *Omni* article goes on to point out that "Brooklyn's oily miracle is just the latest eruption in a volcanic surge of miraculous events and apparitions involving the Virgin Mary," indicating that a "tremendous longing for religious experience—for firsthand contact with the miraculous and the divine . . . is driving people across the country to sites like Bensenhurst." *Omni's* article states that many people have been having visions of the Virgin and mentions some of the better-known alleged appearances across North America and in other parts of the world. Some have occurred in well-to-do neighborhoods, prompting *Omni* to comment that "middle-class Americans . . . cannot reconcile the worldly, skeptical, scientific, conscious parts of their minds with their deeply emotional religious longings and fears."

Above all else, you and I must understand that the issue in the story about the weeping icon is not rational proof. It's belief. It's the human need for *more* than a rational, scientific explanation for everything in life. It's a profound need for the spiritual.

Paradigm shift

That need is exploding in our Western society. It's called a "paradigm shift."

A paradigm is the basic way we explain reality. Two of the most common ways are rational-scientific explanations and religious-supernatural explanations. A paradigm shift occurs when a society changes the way it explains reality. For the past several hundred years, Western thought has increasingly been based on rational-scientific explanations of reality, but a paradigm shift is going on in our society even as you read this book. And that's the point of the story about the weeping icon. The problem with New York's TV anchorman is not his skepticism that the oily tears are supernatural. It's that he fails to see in the humble priest's faith something more than mere gullibility. The newscaster fails to realize that the society he's so accustomed to, in which logic and science reign supreme, is on the way out.

THE COMING GREAT CALAMITY

Individual humans sometimes change their paradigms quickly. This happens, for example, when a scientist becomes a Christian. This doesn't mean that the scientist gives up all the scientific assumptions he has grown so accustomed to. It means that science is no longer the only way or perhaps even the most important way that he explains reality.

Societies change much more slowly. A paradigm shift for an entire culture may take several hundred years. At least that has been the case in the past.

Hellenism

Two thousand years ago, Hellenism had dominated people's thinking throughout the Mediterranean world for several hundred years. Hellenism was humanity's best effort up to that time to develop a rational basis for determining reality.

However, by the time Christ came into the world, a major paradigm shift was already underway. Ellen White describes it well in her book *The Desire of Ages*.

> "When the fullness of the time was come, God sent forth His Son." Providence had directed the movements of nations, and the tide of human impulse and influence, until the world was ripe for the coming of the Deliverer. The nations were united under one government. One language was widely spoken, and was everywhere recognized as the language of literature. . . .
>
> At this time the systems of heathenism were losing their hold upon the people. Men were weary of pageant and fable. They longed for a religion that could satisfy the heart. While the light of truth seemed to have departed from among men, there were souls

who were looking for light, and who were filled with perplexity and sorrow. They were thirsting for a knowledge of the living God, for some assurance of a life beyond the grave (*The Desire of Ages*, 32).

Notice the interest in spirituality that Ellen White says was growing at the time Christ came into the world two thousand years ago. Numerous cults with initiation rites and secret mysteries were taking hold of people's minds at this time. One of the best known of these was Mithraism. Ellen White put her finger on one of the major reasons why these cults were so popular: People "longed for a religion that could satisfy the heart. . . . They were thirsting for a knowledge of the living God, for some assurance of a life beyond the grave."

Another "cult" at that time was Christianity,* which, like Mithraism, had a cleansing initiation rite (baptism) and a secret mystery (communion). You and I understand that Christianity offered the only true solution to these longings, and that's why God chose this period of history—when people were searching for truth—to plant His new Christian religion.

Eventually, Christianity conquered the Roman Empire, and the paradigm shift was complete. For the next twelve hundred years religion, and specifically the Christian religion, was the dominant mode of thought throughout the European world. Islam conquered Christianity in the Middle East and northern Africa, but it was also a religion. Thus, the entire Mediterranean world was dominated by religious thought patterns throughout most of the first millennium and the first half of the second.

The Renaissance

The Renaissance changed all that. In 1510 Copernicus announced that our globe was just one of several planets that orbited the sun, and our world was not the center of the universe. All thought patterns die hard, of course, and the religious way of thinking that had ruled for nearly a millennium and a half was no exception. The church fought the new knowledge with a vengeance. About one hundred and twenty years after Copernicus's announcement, Galileo was forced to recant this scientific reality in a church court.

However, no authority, regardless of how long it has dominated people's minds, can keep them from changing once they begin to understand reality according to a different paradigm. By the beginning of the twentieth century, science (or scientism) held a firm grip on Western thought patterns. Another name for this mode of thought is *secularism*, or, as it is often called, "secular humanism." And, increasingly, people throughout the world began explaining reality primarily in rational, secular terms rather than from a religious viewpoint.

Even Christianity, which claims to base its conclusions on the supernatural, has been profoundly affected by the rational, secular, scientific paradigm. For example, when your doctor is puzzled about what ails you, do you expect him to consult the Bible or his medical books for the answer? What kind of books do you think your mechanic read as he was taking his training? And granted that in our Adventist culture we want the Bible to be the basic textbook in education, which book do you expect your son or daughter to study in college if he or she majors in chemistry or physics?

This secular paradigm pervades our lives today in ways we don't even realize. We expect the major institutions of our culture to be secular: public education, communications (news, books, magazines), entertainment, government, etc. I realized how much this secular paradigm has affected my own thinking one day when I was reading a secular women's magazine in a doctor's waiting room. As I leafed through the magazine, I came to an advertisement for a religious product, and I got the strangest feeling that this advertisement didn't belong in this magazine. I had to stop and make myself realize that a religious manufacturer had as much right to advertise in this magazine as anyone.

This secular, scientific mind-set has dominated Western culture during my entire lifetime and the lifetime of my parents and grandparents. Most people would probably feel comfortable with the idea that it reached its peak during the middle of the twentieth century with the explosion of the atomic bomb over Japan in 1945 and the Apollo moon landing in 1969.

The age of Aquarius

I find it extremely significant, however, that the next major paradigm shift in Western society was under way even as Neil Armstrong took his first step on the moon. The hippie movement of the 1960s may seem like a poor candidate for the distinction of leading the way into the next paradigm shift, but that's exactly what happened. For, if we define spirituality as life based on intuition and "inner light" as opposed to rationalism, then the hippie movement was profoundly spiritual. It was also a rebellion against scientism and an affirmation of values other than money and technology—two of the hallmarks of the rational-scientific paradigm.

New Age spiritualism is another evidence of the profound paradigm shift that is underway even as you read these words. Conservative Christians believe the New Age to be false, but that's beside the point in this discussion. What matters is that the New Age also rejects science and technology as the only source of truth. New Age enthusiasts believe that the age of Pisces is giving way to the age of Aquarius, which they claim will be characterized by worldwide peace.

The Twelve-Step recovery movement is yet another evidence that we are entering an age that emphasizes spirituality as much as rationalism. This movement began in the late 1930s with a group of alcoholics in Akron, Ohio. However, during its first twenty or thirty years, it was confined to alcoholics. Only in the last twenty to thirty years has it become widely accepted as a way to overcome a large variety of compulsive-obsessive behaviors. And this spiritually-centered movement that is not tied to any one religion has flourished during the same years that New Age spiritual ideas have been catching the attention of the whole world.

So-called out-of-body experiences are yet another evidence of the increasing importance westerners at the end of the twentieth century are placing on spirituality at the expense of rationalism. Interest in angels and appearances of the Virgin Mary also fit in as evidences of the paradigm shift.

A development that has captured the attention of Seventh-day Adventists in North America is the growing influence of the Religious Right, of which the Christian Coalition is the most obvious expression. The increasing popularity of conservative talk-radio programs such as that of Rush Limbaugh goes hand in hand with the growth in power of the Religious Right. And on a worldwide basis, we see the Roman Catholic Church emerging as the world's moral policeman. On certain moral issues, even fundamentalist Muslims are joining hands with them!

Yes, a paradigm shift of major proportions is going on in the whole world, not just the West. The shift is away from secular authorities and secular ways of understanding reality to spiritual authorities and spiritual ways of explaining reality.

Please pay careful attention to what I say next because I believe it is one of the most significant evidences that we live in the end time. God chose the time when a major paradigm shift was occurring in Western society to send His Son into the world the first time. The evidence suggests that He has chosen a similar time to send His Son into the world the second time.

---

* It sounds offensive to us to call Christianity a cult. However, the general populace of the first century A.D. thought of Christianity as a cult.

CHAPTER TWO

GOD'S WEAPONS

Take a trip with me, would you. We're going to go back in time—back beyond the birth of Jesus, back before Daniel, back before David, back even before Jacob. We're going to go back to the time of Abraham. However, we won't be visiting with Abraham. On this trip we're going down to Sodom to get acquainted with Brother Lot.

In fact, let's sit in for Brother Lot and his wife. Let's pretend that we are them, they are us.

We're sitting at the city gate one hot evening in mid-summer watching the whirlwinds blow up funnels of dust in the desert. Presently our eyes catch sight of two figures in the distance. They're coming toward us on the road that leads to the city, and as they come near, we can tell that they are strangers.

In the good tradition of desert dwellers of that region, we invite them to stay in our home, and though at first they refuse, we finally persuade them to come with us.

After supper, sitting around the table chatting with them, we're impressed with how gracious they are. They seem to be the friendliest people we've ever met. We wish that our own town had more people like them. We urge them to stay and make their home in our community, but at this suggestion, our new friends become strangely quiet. They exchange apprehensive glances, and for the first time we feel uneasy around them.

When we ask if something's wrong, one of them clears his throat, as though to say something, and then he pauses, fingering the cloth on the table. Both of them are silent for a long time. Somehow we have the feeling that we shouldn't say anything, though, so we sit and wait. Finally, one of them speaks up.

"God is going to destroy this city," he says.

We jump up from our chairs. "When?" we ask.

Looking us straight in the eye, our guest says, "Tomorrow."

"How?" we ask. "What is He going to do?"

But our guest is silent. He says only one thing: "Warn all your family throughout the city to flee for their lives the very first thing in the morning. They must not delay."

It's nearly midnight by now, but we rush outside and down the street. Reaching the home of our son, we bang on the door. A moment later we hear his voice: "Who is it?"

"It's us—Dad and Mom," we cry. "Open up. We must tell you something. It's terribly urgent!"

We push through the door the instant he cracks it open. "Son, get your family out of this city! God is going to destroy it tomorrow."

Our son's mouth drops open, and he takes a step back. "Mom, Dad, are you out of your minds? Where did you hear such a stupid thing?"

THE COMING GREAT CALAMITY

We point back down the street. "The strangers who are staying with us. They told us."

Our son looks at the floor and shakes his head, and then, with his eyes still on the floor, he lets out a sigh and rubs his forehead with his fingers. A moment later he looks at us with a condescending smile. "Dad," he says, "I told you not to take those crazies in. They're out of their minds. This city is perfectly safe!"

We beg and plead, we argue for half an hour, but it's no use. Our son is convinced that we've become religious fanatics. Finally we leave and go to the home of our oldest daughter and her husband. The response is the same. Dad and Mom have lost their minds. Each of our five children who've left home tell us we're crazy and they have no intention of leaving the city just because a couple of complete strangers tell us God is going to destroy the place.

By morning the whole city has heard the news, and everyone is laughing. They are practically in hysterics by the time the strangers take us by the hand and drag us out of town. Half a mile down the road we can still hear their faint laughter.

But the strangers don't give us time to listen. "Escape for your lives!" they shout. "Don't look back."

Half an hour later we hear a deafening roar, and we know that the warning the strangers gave us is true. Our hearts ache for our children and their families, but we have to keep pushing on.

Does the story of Sodom seem more real to you now? I hope so. However, let's not stop our imaginings quite yet. In our imaginations, let's return to Sodom, arriving the very instant the fire and brimstone strike. What would we hear the people say? How must they have felt the few seconds or perhaps moments after the fire fell? What thoughts went through their minds? Of one thing we can be sure: They weren't laughing. No, no! They were terribly, painfully aware that the warning they had received the night before was absolutely right. Suddenly, the God of Lot, whom they had scorned all these years, turned out to be fully in control, exactly as Lot had told them He was.

Do you suppose that Lot and his wife wondered whether the angels' warning might be a big joke? Were they tempted to feel a bit foolish as the angels dragged them through the jeering crowd? The sky overhead was blue and the clouds were drifting along. There wasn't a sign of trouble anywhere, yet the angels were shouting danger at the top of their lungs. And everyone but Lot and his family stood around laughing. They were fleeing this supposed danger at the very time when the rest of their world was settling down for another day of business as usual.

Yes, I'm sure that Lot and his family felt foolish. I'm sure they wondered whether it was really true. And you and I would probably have felt the same, had we been in their place. But they gave the warning, and they followed through on it themselves. And God spared them from the disaster.

God's weapons

God could have used the army of a foreign nation to destroy Sodom and Gomorrah. In fact, He had allowed this to happen a few years earlier, perhaps as a warning (see Genesis 14:1-24). In doing so, He could have stood behind the scenes, using what to human eyes appeared to be just the normal outworking of human events to achieve His purpose. Except for their interaction with Lot and Abraham, who rescued them, the people of Sodom and Gomorrah were unaware of God's part in the over-

17

throw and reestablishment of their city. God usually works out His will in the world through such natural events.

But on a few occasions, God has chosen to bring about His purpose by confronting human beings directly with His own weapons.

God's weapons? you say.

Yes. Didn't you know that God has weapons? Let me tell you about them. His weapons are the forces of nature. For example, God said to Job:

> Have you entered the storehouses of the snow
> > or seen the storehouses
> > > of the hail,
> > *which I reserve* for times of
> > > trouble,
> > > *for days of war and battle?*
> > > > (Job 38:22, 23).

God said He uses the forces of nature as weapons for battle. This is often evident in the psalms:

> The earth trembled and
> > quaked,
> > and the foundations of
> > > the mountains
> > > shook;
> > they trembled because he was angry. . . .
> He made darkness his covering,
> > his canopy
> > around him—
> the dark rain clouds of the sky.
> *Out of the brightness of his*
> > *presence clouds advanced,*
> *with hailstones and bolts of*

lightning.
The Lord thundered from
heaven;
 the voice of the Most High resounded.
He shot his arrows and
   scattered the
   enemies,
  great bolts of lightning and routed them.
The valleys of the sea were
exposed
 and the foundations of
   the earth laid
   bare
at your rebuke, O Lord,
 at the blast of breath from your nostrils
    (Psalm 18:7, 11-15).

A similar description is found in Isaiah 29:5-7. Notice, again, that God uses the forces of nature against the wicked who are attacking Ariel, that is, Jerusalem:[1]

Suddenly, in an instant,
 the Lord Almighty will come
with thunder and earthquake
   and great noise,
with windstorm and
   tempest and flames
   of a devouring
   fire.
Then the hordes of all the
nations that fight against
Ariel,
 that attack her and her
   fortress and

19

> besiege her,
> will be as it is with a dream,
> with a vision in the night.

"Oh, God is just speaking metaphorically in these verses," you say.

Since we today have never seen God actually use the elements in this way, it's easy for us to suppose that these passages in the psalms and the prophets are just metaphors. However, a brief look at biblical history helps us to understand that in those moments when God has intervened most dramatically and powerfully in human affairs, He has used the forces of nature to accomplish His purpose.

Take the story we were just considering. The Bible says that God "rained down burning sulphur" (KJV: fire and brimstone) on the cities of the plain, and they were consumed.(See Gen. 19:24.) Ellen White makes an interesting comment on this event:

> As the sun arose for the last time upon the cities of the plain, the people thought to commence another day of godless riot. All were eagerly planning their business or their pleasure, and the messenger of God was derided for his fears and his warnings. Suddenly as the thunder peal from an unclouded sky, fell balls of fire on the doomed capital (*Seventh-day Adventist Bible Commentary*, 5:1122).

We don't know whether these "balls of fire" were brought about by some known cause such as a volcano or meteorites, or whether God bypassed the usual forces of nature and produced the balls of fire "miraculously." However, the passages we just read from the Bible suggest that His most common method is to direct the forces of nature that already exist in the universe. This was surely the case in two other dramatic events in Bible history.

Egypt and the Exodus

When Jacob went to Egypt to be near his son Joseph, God allowed their descendants to remain there for many years. By the time God was ready to replant them in the land of Canaan, however, they had been enslaved by a powerful pharaoh who did not want to let them go. God could have brought some other nation against the pharaoh to defeat him, but again, He chose to use the forces of nature.

It is hardly necessary for me to recount the story for you. Ten terrible plagues fell on the land, leaving Egypt a wasteland. By the time God was through, the crops had all been destroyed, a storm had ripped up many of the buildings, disease had claimed the lives of most of the cattle, and the firstborn son in every family was dead.

But God's purpose was accomplished. He delivered His people from the pharaoh's power and sent them on their journey to a new land. When the pharaoh and his army set off after the Israelites to bring them back into slavery, God again used the forces of nature to deliver His people. He caused the Red Sea to part just long enough for the Israelites to escape to the other side, and then He brought the waters of the sea back upon the Egyptians and drowned them.

The Flood

By far the most outstanding biblical example of God's intervention in human affairs with the forces of nature is the Flood of Noah, which, according to biblical chronology, occurred a little less than five thousand years ago. The Bible says that all the springs of the great deep burst forth, and the floodgates of the heavens were opened. These are events of nature, used by God to bring about the destruction of a sinful world that had gotten morally out of control.

I have no doubt that had today's scientists lived at the time of the Flood, and had they had access to twentieth-century technology, they could have told us exactly what caused the springs of the great deep to burst forth and the floodgates of the heavens to open. The bursting forth of the springs of the great deep suggests that a worldwide earthquake broke up the earth's underground water systems, allowing the waters to flood the earth. Ellen White spoke of "jets of water" that "burst from the earth with indescribable force," throwing huge rocks "hundreds of feet into the air" (*Patriarchs and Prophets*, 99).

It's difficult to even speculate what might have precipitated the condensation of massive amounts of water in the atmosphere, causing it to add to the flooding of the earth. The Bible only says that it happened. It does not say why. It's entirely possible that a single event caused both the earthquake and the condensation of water in the atmosphere.

The one thing of which we can be certain is this: At the time of the Flood, God used the powerful forces of nature to accomplish His will. He used natural phenomena to destroy the works of sinful human beings. He used His weapons of warfare.

---

1. See *The Seventh-day Adventist Bible Commentary*, 4:214, comment under Isaiah 29:1.

CHAPTER THREE

THE COMING JUDGMENTS
of God

Gd is about to intervene again with His weapons of warfare. I am speaking about the second coming of Christ and the events that will lead up to it.

Few Seventh-day Adventists have any idea of the severity of the crisis that faces the world. Horrible natural disasters will fall on our planet, making the disasters we are familiar with pale into insignificance. If we are ignorant of these things, Ellen White was not. She had no doubt about the terrible nature of the disasters that will come upon the world in the final days of earth's history.

I suspect that our ignorance is largely due to two factors. First, Ellen White never wrote an entire book or even an entire chapter about these disasters. We have to pick out her statements about coming natural disasters from here and there in her writings and bring them together ourselves in order to get a comprehensive view. But so far as I know, nobody has ever done that.[1] This chapter is a partial effort in that direction.

Second, Ellen White seems to have developed a special burden for this subject around 1895 that continued at least through 1905. God showed her more about the nature and extent of the coming natural disasters during this period than He ever had before. However, the first edition of her magnum opus on end-time events—*The Great Controversy*—was published in 1888, a number of years before God began revealing to her more fully the extent of the disasters to come. Had she been aware of these future judgments at the time she wrote *The Great Controversy*, I have no doubt that she would have said a great deal about them. Since she did not comment on them in *The Great Controversy*, we have remained largely unaware of them.

In this chapter, we will review some of Ellen White's more definitive statements about the coming disasters. My purpose in sharing these statements with you is to give you an idea of the magnitude of the crisis that faces us. I will divide her comments into several categories.

A terrible crisis is coming

Ellen White wrote urgently during the final years of her life that a terrible crisis is coming upon the world:

> We are standing on the threshold of the crisis of the ages. In quick succession the judgments of God will follow one another—fire, and flood, and earthquake, with war and bloodshed (*Prophets and Kings*, 278).

Notice that after referring to the "crisis of the ages," Ellen White went on to describe the nature of that crisis as natural disasters: "Judgments of God [that will] follow one another—fire, and flood, and earthquake, with war and bloodshed." These are God's weapons of warfare!

Here is an interesting statement with significant implications about natural disasters as God's weapons of war:

> The armory of heaven is open; all the universe of God and its equipments are ready. One word has justice to speak, and there will be terrific representations upon the earth, of the wrath of God. There will be voices and thunderings and lightnings and earthquakes and universal desolation. Every movement in the universe of heaven is to prepare the world for the great crisis (*Special Testimonies*, Series A, 1b:38).

The opening sentence in this statement is particularly significant. Ellen White says that "the armory of heaven is open." An armory is a storehouse for weapons. God's weapons, as we saw in the previous chapter, are the forces of nature, and Ellen White names the weapons in God's armory as "thunders and lightnings and earthquakes," which she says will cause "universal desolation."

After speaking of God's armory, Ellen White says that "all the universe of God and its equipments are ready." The "universe of God" is almost certainly a reference to the loyal inhabitants of the universe outside of our world, including the angels. I would understand the "equipments" of this universe to be the weapons stored in God's armory.

Ellen concludes this paragraph by saying that "every movement in the universe of heaven is to prepare the world for the great crisis." This "great crisis" is, without a doubt, the "crisis of the ages" that we read about in the previous statement. It will obviously be caused by the weapons in God's armory, when He and His angels make use of their "equipments."

Thus it is very clear that God's weapons—the destructive forces of nature—will be key elements in creating the coming world crisis.

A series of disasters

Ellen White also understood that this crisis will be precipitated by many natural disasters, not just one or two. We already saw this in her statement from *Prophets and Kings* that "in quick succession the judgments of God will follow one another." The following statements echo the same theme:

> God cannot forbear much longer. Already His judgments are beginning to fall on some places, and soon His signal displeasure will be felt in other places.
>
> There will be *a series of events* revealing that God is master of the situation (*Testimonies for the Church*, 9:96).

Notice first that Ellen White began this statement by calling attention to the judgments of God that were already falling on the world "in some places" at her time. Then she said that "soon His signal displeasure will be felt in other places." In this context it is evident that the coming "series of events" that she predicted will also be natural disasters. And her expression "series of events" leaves no doubt that there will be many disasters, not just one or two.

She also says that these disasters will reveal "that God is master of the situation." Most readers probably remember the dramatic events during the last half of 1989, when the nations of eastern Europe broke away from Communism and domination by the Soviet Union. This was clearly "a series of events," and I can still remember reading in Adventist magazines that these events signaled God's control over the affairs of the nations. A similar series of events—natural disasters this time—will again reveal that God is in control of the world.

Here is another statement suggesting that more than one natural disaster will be involved in the final crisis:

> When the crisis is upon us, when the season of calamity shall come, they [souls from other churches] will come to the front, gird themselves with the whole armor of God, and exalt His law (*Selected Messages*, 3:387).

This statement begins with a reference to "the crisis." Ellen White is almost certainly referring to the final crisis that we noted in the previous section. Now notice the first two clauses: "When the crisis is upon us, when the season of calamity shall come . . ." I will not trouble you with the details about the grammatical structure of these clauses. However, even a casual glance makes it clear that the crisis and the season of calamity are the same thing.

A season is a short period of time. Thus a short time is coming during which calamities will be coming upon the earth. Even now we see calamities occurring all over the world, but nothing that we would characterize as "a season of calamity." I believe that when this season of calamity comes, all God's people, and indeed the world as a whole, will recognize it.

The following statement makes it absolutely clear that a time of multiple calamities is coming: "Calamities will come—calamities most awful, most unexpected; and these destructions will follow one after another" (*Evangelism*, 27).

Ellen White begins this statement by pointing out that "calamities most awful" will come upon the world, and then she says that "these destructions will follow one after another." Again, we are to understand that in the coming crisis there will be many judgments of God, not just one or two.

Nature of the coming disasters

What kind of disasters can we expect during this time? To a great extent, the same as the ones the world is experiencing right now but in much greater intensity. Ellen White spoke of earthquakes, volcanoes, famines, epidemics, and tidal waves, among others.

earthquakes Terrible shocks will come upon the earth, and the lordly palaces erected at great expense will certainly become heaps of ruins. The earth's crust will be rent by the outbursts of the elements concealed in the bowels of the earth (*Selected Messages*, 3:391). *volcanoes*

The "terrible shocks" that Ellen White spoke about probably refer to earthquakes, particularly in view of the fact that they will cause "the lordly palaces erected at great expense" to become "heaps of ruins." And her comment that the earth's crust will be rent by the outbursts of "the elements concealed in the bowels of the earth" seems quite clearly to refer to volcanoes.[2]

In the last scenes of this earth's history, war will rage. There will be pestilence, plague, and famine. The waters of the deep will overflow their boundaries. Property and life will be destroyed by fire and flood (*Review and Herald*, 19 Oct. 1897; *Maranatha*, 174).

The first sentence in this statement mentions war, epidemics ("pestilence" and "plague"), and famine. Ellen White then makes a most interesting comment. She says that "the waters of the deep will overflow their boundaries." The "waters of the deep" are the oceans, and their "boundaries" are the seacoasts. The name for the disaster that is caused by the ocean overflowing its coastlands is "tidal wave" or "tsunami" (the Japanese word for tidal wave).

Ellen White spoke of tidal waves at the end of time on at least two occasions. Here is the other one:

> "And there shall be signs in the sun, and in the moon, and in the stars; and upon the earth distress of nations, with perplexity, the sea and the waves roaring" (Luke 21:25). Yes, they [the sea and the waves] shall pass their borders, and destruction will be in their track (*Selected Messages*, 3:417). *The tidal wave in Indonesia*

Terrible calamities coming on the cities

Ellen White especially called attention to the cities as the focus of God's judgments in the end time. The following statements are just a few of the many that I could share with you:

> Cities full of transgression, and sinful in the extreme, will be destroyed by earthquakes, by fire, by flood (*Evangelism*, 27).

> The time is near when large cities will be swept away (ibid., 29).

THE COMING GREAT CALAMITY

> O that God's people had a sense of the
> impending destruction of thousands of cities, now
> almost given to idolatry (ibid., 29).

Notice that in the last statement above Ellen White said that "thousands of cities" will be destroyed. "Thousands" (plural) suggests at least two thousand. Hurricane Andrew, which struck the coasts of Florida and Louisiana in 1993, was the most costly hurricane in U.S. history, yet it destroyed only one small city—Homestead, Florida. This naturally leads to the question, What kind of disaster or disasters will it take to destroy two thousand or more cities? *also New Orleans*

Judgments of God before the close of probation

One of the most significant questions we can ask is whether these judgments of God will occur before or after the close of probation. In the past, many Adventists, reading Ellen White's statements quoted above, probably assumed that she was describing events that would occur during the seven last plagues. This, of course, would be after the close of probation. However, the evidence from her writings leaves us in no doubt that many of these judgments will occur before the close of probation. We have already seen the first part of the following statement once in this chapter. Here it is again, but carried further to help us understand when these judgments of God will occur in relation to the close of probation:

> Calamities will come—calamities most awful,
> most unexpected; and these destructions will
> follow one after another. . . . Strictly will the
> cities of the nations be dealt with, and yet they
> will not be visited in the extreme of God's

indignation, because some souls will yet break away from the delusions of the enemy, and will repent and be converted, while the mass will be treasuring up wrath against the day of wrath (ibid., 27).

Notice that the context of this statement is the time when calamities "most awful, most unexpected" will be coming on the world "one after another." This is unquestionably the time of the final crisis—the season of calamity that we read about earlier, when "a series of events" will reveal that God is "master of the situation." Next, notice that she says that as a result of these terrible judgments, "some souls will yet break away from the delusions of the enemy, and will repent and be converted." We have to place the time she speaks of before the close of probation, because no one will transfer from Satan's side to God's side after the close of probation.

Two kinds of calamities will come upon the world as judgments from God at the end of time. The first will be *warning* judgments. These will occur before the close of probation. They will be God's effort to wake up the human race and call their attention to the approaching close of probation and the end of the world. These judgments will be God's last call to humanity, His final invitation for men and women to accept Jesus as their Saviour and win eternal life. This is the time when God's people will proclaim the final warning and the loud cry.

The second kind of calamity will be the terrible wrath of God the third angel's message warns about. The purpose of these judgments will be *punishment*. The Bible calls them "the seven last plagues," and they will occur after the close of probation.

In this book, we will not be discussing the seven last

THE COMING GREAT CALAMITY

plagues except in passing. The focus of this book is the warning judgments of God before the close of probation.

The following statement is composed of two rather long sentences. Earlier in this chapter we used the second sentence to show that a "season of calamity" is coming during which God's judgments will be falling on the earth. By including the sentence that immediately precedes it, we can locate this season of calamity before the close of probation:

> There are many souls to come out of the ranks of the world, out of the churches—even the Catholic Church—whose zeal will far exceed that of those who have stood in the rank and file to proclaim the truth heretofore. . . . When the crisis is upon us, when the season of calamity shall come, they will come to the front, gird themselves with the whole armor of God, and exalt His law (*Selected Messages*, 3:386, 387).

We noted earlier that the season of calamity is a short time during which natural disasters will be coming on the world and that Ellen White identified this season of calamity as the final crisis. Thus there can be no doubt that both the "season of calamity" and the final crisis will begin before the close of probation, because at that time people will be coming out of the other churches to join with God's people. This cannot happen after the close of probation. In this statement Ellen White also calls our attention to the fact that many of those who accept our message in the final crisis will join with us in proclaiming that message.

The following statement also locates "the time of God's destructive judgments" before the close of probation:

(The time of God's destructive judgments is the time of mercy for those who have [had] no opportunity to learn what is truth.) Tenderly will the Lord look upon them. His heart of mercy is touched; *His hand is still stretched out to save,* while the door is closed to those who would not enter (*Testimonies for the Church,* 9:97, emphasis supplied).

Notice that at the time of God's destructive judgments— the season of calamity when a "series of events" will reveal that God is master of the situation—God's hand is still stretched out to save. Again, we are compelled to locate this time before the close of probation.

The following diagram illustrates what we have learned up to this point about the final crisis, the close of probation, and the second coming of Christ:

The crisis begins	The close of probation	Second coming of Christ
Warning judgments	Punishing judgments	
THE FINAL CRISIS		

This, I believe, is an accurate representation of Ellen White's understanding that the final crisis will begin before the close of probation, and that it will extend beyond the close of probation to the second coming of Christ.

Calamities will be sudden

Several times in her writings, Ellen White called attention to the fact that the judgments of God will come upon the world very suddenly. We will examine the following statement for the third time in this chapter:

THE COMING GREAT CALAMITY

Calamities will come—calamities most awful, most unexpected; and these destructions will follow one after another (*Evangelism*, 27).

Notice that these calamities will be "most unexpected." Later in this book we will discover the significance of the surprise element in these disasters. The following statement, though it does not mention natural disasters or judgments from God, does convey the idea of surprise:

The work of the people of God is to prepare for the events of the future, which will soon come upon them with blinding force (*Selected Messages*, 2:142).

Let's break in here to notice a very significant statement in the Bible about the suddenness of God's coming judgments. Paul warned Christians to expect sudden judgments from God. He said, "While people are saying, 'Peace and safety,' destruction will come on them *suddenly*, as labor pains on a pregnant woman" (1 Thessalonians 5:3).

Most Adventists who quote Paul's words stop here. However, notice what Paul says next: "But you, brothers, are not in darkness so that this day should surprise you like a thief" (verse 4). In other words, God's people are to be aware of the sudden and terrible judgments of God that are coming on the world. No wonder Ellen White warned us over and over about them!

In my opinion, Ellen White's most striking statement about the suddenness of the coming judgments of God is found on page 412 of *Christ's Object Lessons*. Page 412 is part of the chapter in which she comments on Jesus' parable of the ten virgins. The paragraph in question is fairly long, so I will break it into two parts. Here is the first part:

It is in a crisis that character is revealed. When the earnest voice proclaimed at midnight, "Behold the bridegroom cometh; go ye out to meet him," and the sleeping virgins were roused from their slumbers, it was seen who had made preparation for the event. Both parties were taken unawares; but one was prepared for the emergency, and the other was found without preparation.

Ellen White is commenting about a very specific time in the story of the ten virgins—the moment when they were awakened. They did not wake up naturally. They were awakened by a "midnight cry" that the bridegroom was on the way. This midnight cry precipitated a crisis among the virgins when half of them discovered that they were unprepared for the arrival of the bridegroom.

I will quote the rest of the paragraph in a moment, but let's begin by looking at just the first two words that follow the portion quoted above: "So now . . ." It is obvious that Ellen White is going to apply the message of the ten virgins to our time, and she will especially comment on the midnight cry that woke them up. The ten virgins represent God's church, and the midnight cry that woke them up represents the church's wake-up call. By saying "so now," Ellen White is preparing to apply the wake-up call of the ten virgins to God's church today. And this, she says, will precipitate a crisis for God's people, just as it did for the ten virgins.

Now notice what will be the nature of this wake-up call for God's sleeping saints in our time:

So now, *a sudden and unlooked-for calamity*, something that brings the soul face to face with death, will show whether there is any real faith in

Kay

the promises of God. It will show whether the soul is sustained by grace. The great final test comes at the close of human probation, when it will be too late for the soul's need to be supplied[3] (ibid., 412, emphasis supplied).

Let's take a moment to compare this statement with one from *Evangelism,* page 27, that we examined earlier:

- "Calamities will come—calamities most awful, most unexpected."
- "So now, a sudden and unlooked-for calamity . . ." (*Christ's Object Lessons*, 412).

Notice the following similarities between these statements:

Evangelism	Christ's Object Lessons
Calamities	Calamity
Most awful	"Terrible" is implied
Most unexpected	Sudden, unlooked for

That both statements speak of calamities is so obvious as to hardly require further comment. We do need to notice one difference between them though. The statement in *Evangelism* speaks of calamities in the plural while in *Christ's Object Lessons* the calamity is singular—"*a* calamity." This is not a contradiction, however. In order to have a "series of" calamities that will follow "one after another," there must be a first one in the series. I suggest that Ellen White's statement in *Christ's Object Lessons* refers to only the first one in the series. This is appropriate, since the context is about the wake-up call of the sleeping virgins. Presumably by the time the second and third calamities occur, the virgins will have awakened.

Ellen White goes on to say that this calamity will be "sudden" and "unlooked for"—that is, unexpected. Apparently the human race will be taken by surprise.

We now need to ask a couple of questions about this calamity. Ellen White likens it to the midnight cry that awakened the virgins in Christ's parable. The first question, then, is this: Where are the ten virgins today? Ellen White helps us to answer that question by the way she interprets the parable: "Christ . . . told His disciples the parable of the ten virgins, by their experience illustrating the experience of the church that shall live just before His second coming" (*Christ's Object Lessons*, 406). In other words, the virgins represent the church universal at the time of Christ's coming. Thus the answer to the question of where these virgins are today is simple: They are all over the world.

The answer to the first question leads us immediately to the second: What kind of calamity will it take to awaken God's people all over the world at one time? This is an impossible question to answer, of course, other than to say that it will have to exceed any calamity that has occurred in recorded history other than the Flood of Noah.

Hurricane Andrew, in 1993, was the most destructive hurricane in U.S. history, but it hardly awakened the church all over the world. Neither did the earthquakes in southern California and Kobe, Japan, in 1995, nor did the floods in the midwest in 1994 or the firestorms in Los Angeles and Sydney that same year. None of the calamities the human race has experienced in the last 100 years has awakened the sleeping saints all over the world.

So whatever this calamity is, it is still future.

A change in God's dealings

In numerous places Ellen White makes it clear that

there is coming a change in God's dealings with the world. Here are three representative statements:

> In the exercise of the longsuffering of God, He gives to nations a certain period of probation, but there is a point which, if they pass, there will be the visitation of God in His indignation (*Selected Messages*, 3:396).

In this statement, Ellen White applied the principle of God's judgments to nations. However, the same principle applies to the world as a whole, as the following statements make clear, especially the second one:

> The angel that stood by my side declared that the Lord has appointed a time when He will visit transgressors in wrath for persistent disregard of His law (*Testimonies for the Church*, 9:93).

> Do you believe that the Lord is coming, and that the last great crisis is about to break upon the world? There will soon come a change in God's dealings. The world in its perversity is being visited by casualties,—by floods, storms, fires, earthquakes, famines, wars, and bloodshed. The Lord is slow to anger and great in power; but His forbearance will not always continue. Who is prepared for the sudden change that will take place in God's dealings with sinful men? (*Fundamentals of Christian Education*, 356, 357).

This last statement makes it very clear that God had not yet changed His attitude—His dealings—with the human race at the time Ellen White wrote it, and I believe that He still has not. At the time I am writing these words in mid-1995, He is still withholding his terrible judgments. I believe that the final crisis will begin at the time when these judgments begin to fall, before the close of probation. The purpose of God's judgments at this time will be to warn the human race that their opportunity to repent and accept Christ as Saviour is almost over, that time is running out.

---

1. I brought together some of these statements in chapter 8 of my book *The Crisis of the End Time*. However, that chapter only touched on the highlights, and even in the present chapter I will not review all the evidence available from Ellen White's writings on the coming natural disasters.
2. See also *The Seventh-day Adventist Bible Commentary*, 7:946—a statement about volcanoes that probably refers to events that will occur immediately before Christ's second coming.
3. See Appendix B at the end of this book for a further comment on this statement.

CHAPTER FOUR

SIGNS IN THE HEAVENS:
Part 1

Ellen White's predictions about the natural disasters that will immediately precede the second coming of Christ help us to understand that we should expect terrible devastation. The Bible does not say as much about these natural disasters as Ellen White. However, when we compare what the Bible does say with what modern science knows about certain types of natural disaster, we discover that the Bible suggests even greater devastation than Ellen White spoke about.

I will begin by quoting a passage from Matthew 24 that is very familiar to Seventh-day Adventists:

> "Immediately after the distress of those days
> 'the sun will be darkened,
> and the moon will not give its light;
> the stars will fall from the sky,
> and the heavenly bodies will be shaken' "
> (verse 29).

"But the stars fell in 1833, and the dark day happened in 1780!" you say.

That's correct, and I don't wish to challenge that interpretation of Jesus' words here. However, I believe that we have not understood all that they imply. *I agree*

I am sure you are aware that Mark and Luke also give their versions of Jesus' sermon on the signs of the end. Mark's version is almost word-for-word like Matthew's, so we need not concern ourselves with it here. However, Luke adds some significant information that we do not find in the other two gospels. We will begin by reading Luke's words in chapter 21:25, 26:

> "There will be signs in the sun, moon and stars. On the earth, nations will be in anguish and perplexity at the roaring and tossing of the sea. Men will faint from terror, apprehensive of what is coming on the world, for the heavenly bodies will be shaken." *oh, the moon has to do with the tide,*

Let's examine Luke's words a few at a time.

Notice that in the first sentence Luke tells us there will be "signs in the sun, moon and stars," but he does not tell us what those signs will be. Fortunately, Matthew and Mark do tell us. Since all three are quoting from Jesus' same sermon, we are justified in understanding Luke's statement about signs in the sun, moon, and stars to mean the darkening of the sun and the moon and the falling of the stars.

Matthew and Luke did not tell us what the response of the human race will be to these signs, but Luke described it to us quite in detail. According to Luke, Jesus said that "on the earth, nations will be in anguish and perplexity." Notice that the word *nations* is plural—that is, international. We should probably understand Luke to be describing the reaction of the entire human race to these signs.

And what is that response? "Anguish" and "perplexity."

Anguish means "this hurts a lot," and *perplexity* means "what do we do now?" Anguish and perplexity is what you would feel if you were to come home one night and find your house in flames. So the falling of the stars and the darkening of the sun and moon will cause international pain and anguish that will leave the whole world asking, "What do we do now?"

Allow me to ask you two questions. Was there international anguish and perplexity over the dark day in 1780? Was the whole world in anguish and perplexity at the falling of the stars in 1833?

No!

In verse 26 Jesus said that the entire human race will "faint from terror, apprehensive of what is coming on the earth." And what will they be in terror of? The shaking of the heavenly bodies—that is, the signs in the sun, moon, and stars.

Again we need to ask, Was the entire human race in terror over the signs that occurred in 1780 and 1833?

And again the answer is No!

I propose to you that these signs have not yet received their most complete fulfillment.

Does this mean that I reject our traditional understanding of how Jesus' prediction of signs in the sun, moon, and stars was fulfilled? No. I do believe, however, that our pioneers failed to understand all that Jesus meant. They believed the events in 1780 and 1833 meant that the coming of Jesus was imminent, that He would almost certainly come within their lifetime. This obviously did not happen.

Today we can understand what the pioneers could not—that at the time of the end God planned to raise up a movement of people who would scatter all over the world to carry the warning about His soon coming. This movement could not develop within a year or even ten years. As it turns out, the movement has spanned several generations, and this entire period is called "the time of the end."

I believe the signs in the sun, moon, and stars in 1780 and 1833 meant that the time of the end had *begun*, not that it was about to end. Had we lived at the time of the pioneers, we would almost certainly have understood those signs the same way they did. However, reexamining Luke's words 150 years later, we can see in them something the pioneers missed: that these signs were to cause worldwide terror and international anguish and perplexity. Nothing like that occurred in 1780 or 1833. Therefore, I suggest that these signs received only a partial fulfillment back then. Their complete fulfillment is still future, even as I write these words in 1995.

Matthew reports something else Jesus predicted that the pioneers missed but which is extremely significant to our study. We find it in chapter 24:21, 22. Here is what verse 21 says: "For then there will be great distress, unequaled from the beginning of the world until now—and never to be equaled again." These words were not original with Jesus. He was quoting from Daniel 12:1. Here is what Daniel said, with the words Jesus quoted in italics: "At that time Michael, the great prince who protects your people, will arise. *There will be a time of distress such as has not happened from the beginning of nations until then*" (chapter 12:1).

Both Daniel and Jesus pointed forward to a time of distress so terrible that it will exceed anything the world has known since the Flood.[1] This time of distress cannot refer to the 1,260 years of persecution during the Middle

Key

Ages, because it will occur *after* Michael stands up—an action that Adventists have always understood to refer to the close of probation.[2]

Now let's read verse 22: "If those days had not been cut short, no one would survive, but for the sake of the elect those days will be shortened" (verse 22). The original language reads literally, "No flesh would be saved." The Greek word for *saved* is used elsewhere in the New Testament to speak of salvation from sin. However, it should not be understood in that sense here. I believe the New International Version is correct to interpret Jesus to mean "no one would survive."

Please read the following italicized words carefully, because they are extremely important: *Jesus is telling us that the time of distress just before His second coming will be so severe that the human race will be threatened with extinction!* Suddenly, His prediction of natural disasters such as earthquakes, famines, and pestilences take on a new meaning. And, I suggest, so does His prediction about signs in the sun, moon, and stars. For you will recall Luke's prediction that in connection with those signs in the heavens the nations will be in anguish and perplexity, and the human race will be in terror. In other words, the anguish and perplexity of the nations will be over how to save the human race from extinction!

Let me be very specific with you. I believe that the signs in the sun, moon, and stars that Jesus predicted will be fulfilled by comets, asteroids, and/or meteorites. In the next chapter I will elaborate at length on this interpretation of Jesus' prediction, but for now I would like to pause and qualify what I say:

I may be wrong.

In Revelation I thought the sun, moon & stars was following the distress of those days

Immed. after the trib. of those days there would be signs – so there will be another trib.

That's quite a strange statement for an author to make, isn't it? However, in this case I believe it needs to be said, because nobody can be sure exactly what will happen in the future. For example, prior to 1780 and 1833, some Bible students could have claimed that Jesus' prediction of signs in the sun, moon, and stars should be understood symbolically, while others could have argued for a literal fulfillment. As it turns out, the prophecy was fulfilled literally, but until the events actually happened, no one could say for sure that a literal interpretation was correct.

Now that a literal interpretation has been demonstrated to be correct in the partial fulfillment of Jesus' prediction two hundred years ago, we may be on safer ground to expect that its complete fulfillment in the future will also be literal. But we still need to be cautious about interpreting unfulfilled prophecy, because we cannot know what will actually happen until it happens.

Because of this, some people question whether we should try to interpret unfulfilled prophecy at all. My response to that is a bit of advice Jesus gave to His disciples in the upper room the night before His crucifixion: "I have told you now before it happens, so that when it does happen you will believe" (John 14:29). Jesus obviously wanted us to have some idea about what is coming upon the earth, or He would have said nothing at all about signs in the sun, moon, and stars. Peter endorsed the effort to understand unfulfilled prophecy. He said that the Old Testament prophets themselves tried to "find out the time and circumstances to which the Spirit of Christ in them was pointing when he predicted the sufferings of Christ and the glories that would follow" (1 Peter 1:11). So it is appropriate that we should *try* to understand Jesus' prediction about signs in the sun, moon, and stars.

Yet we must recognize that there is a danger in being

too precise in our interpretation of prophecy, and especially in being dogmatic about our preciseness. That was the problem with the Jewish nation at Christ's time. They were so sure of their interpretation of the prophecies about the Messiah's coming that when He came in a different manner than they expected, they rejected Him. So *we must always be willing to recognize that in looking to the future, even through the lens of Bible prophecy, we may be wrong.*

This is what I meant when I said, "I may be wrong."

With this precaution in mind, we are now ready to examine the full implication of Jesus' prediction about signs in the heavens, especially Luke's version. However, since my explanation of these ideas would make the present chapter much too long, we will stop here and begin another chapter.

---

1. Both Jesus and Daniel emphasized that the time of trouble near the end of human history would exceed anything that has happened since there was a nation. The Bible is silent about whether human society was organized into nations before the Flood, but Genesis 10 lists the nations that grew up from Noah's sons after the Flood. Thus, there is good biblical evidence that Daniel and Jesus meant the coming time of trouble will exceed anything the world has known *since the Flood*, not since the beginning of the world.

2. I believe the time of distress that Daniel and Jesus predicted will include the judgments of God before probation's close as well as those after. If this is correct, then Michael's standing up will occur before the close of probation, not at the close of probation.

I need to look up + compare:
Matt, Dan, & Rev. on when:
after the trib of those days?

CHAPTER FIVE

SIGNS IN THE HEAVENS:
Part 2

In July 1994, the cosmos served up a fireworks display that was unprecedented in human history: A large comet broke into half a dozen pieces, and these pieces plunged one-by-one into the planet Jupiter.[1] Scientists might have missed this fiery onslaught altogether—or at least caught it only by chance—had it not been that months before the event they had already observed the comet's fragments diving toward their demise. Thus not only were astronomers and other scientists privileged to get as complete a view as possible of the event;[2] they were able to predict its probable effect on Jupiter.

There was actually some confusion among scientists over exactly what to expect. Some said it would cause only minor damage to the planet. Others believed it would set off a major firestorm. As it turned out, the worst case-scenarios were fully justified, in some cases having underrated what the comet blasts actually did to the planet.

THE COMING GREAT CALAMITY

And because of what happened on Jupiter, the world now knows that the worst-case scenarios predicted by scientists for a similar comet or asteroid invasion on earth are also fully justified. Indeed, the "Jupiter effect" impelled a previously reluctant U.S. Congress to take seriously the threat of an asteroid impact on our planet and what might be done to prevent it.

With this encouraging introduction, let's find out what would happen should planet Earth be struck by a comet, an asteroid, or a large meteorite. I will begin by sharing with you the sources from which I will be quoting. (In the rest of this chapter, I will mention only the names and page numbers of these books and magazines in the references at the end of quotes):

- *National Geographic*, June 1989.
- *Ad Astra*, the magazine of the National Space Society, November/December 1992.
- *Astronomy*, September 1991.
- *Newsweek*, November 23, 1992.
- *Comets, Asteroids, and Meteorites*, Time-Life Books, 1990.
- *The New York Times*, June 15, 1995.
- Clark R. Chapman and David Morrison, *Cosmic Catastrophes*, 1989.

None of these sources are truly scientific. You and I would not understand them if they were. However, this does not make them unreliable. They were written by authors who have the skill to simplify technical and scientific subjects so that people like you and me can understand them.

The cover of *Newsweek's* November 23, 1992, issue tells it all. Beside an illustration of a ball of fire plunging toward planet Earth are the words, "Doomsday Science: New Theories About Comets, Asteroids and How the World Might End."

Adventists and other Christians are not the only ones talking about the end of the world these days! Scientists are in on the act too! And, to add to your comfort, please notice the words of Donald Yeomans, an astronomer with NASA's Jet Propulsion Laboratory in Pasadena, California, that are quoted in *Newsweek's* table of contents blurb: "Earth runs its course about the sun in a swarm of asteroids. . . . *Sooner or later, our planet will be struck by one of them*" (page 3, emphasis added).

wow

Newsweek underscored the proximity of the danger by noting that "on March 23, 1989, an asteroid half a mile across missed Earth by just 700,000 miles. No one saw it coming; if it had arrived a mere six hours later it might have wiped out civilization" (ibid.)

The opening paragraphs in the *Newsweek* article paint a stark picture of what could happen:

> It comes screaming out of the sky like the Scud from hell, bigger than a mountain and packed with more energy than the world's entire nuclear arsenal. It hits the atmosphere at 100 times the velocity of a speeding bullet, and less than a second later smacks into the ground with an explosive force of 100 million megatons of TNT. The shock wave from the crash landing, traveling 20,000 miles an hour, levels everything within 150 miles. Simultaneously a plume of vaporized stone shoots up from the impact site, blasting a hole through the atmosphere and venting hot debris.
>
> The vaporized rock cools, condensing back into hundreds of millions of tiny stones. As they streak

Dan, a stone cut out w/out hands into the image on the feet.

to the ground over the next hour, they heat up, and soon the very air glows pink. Steam hisses from green leaves; buildings and even trees burst into flame. Nitrogen and oxygen in the atmosphere combine into nitric acid; any surviving life crawling out of a burrow or cave, gets pelted with a rain as caustic as the acid in a car battery.

That's what astronomer Henry Melosh of the University of Arizona calculates would happen if something six miles across fell from space and smacked into Earth (56).

Do you think it couldn't happen on our planet? It already has. Scientists today are convinced that an asteroid of this magnitude wiped out most life forms on earth 65 million years ago,[3] including the entire dinosaur population.

But we don't have to go back nearly that far for evidence of meteorite and asteroid activity on earth. Scientists have now concluded that a 1978 explosion in the South Pacific, at first thought to have been caused by an atomic bomb (perhaps a secret Russian experiment), was actually an asteroid. And on June 30, 1908, a fiery blast over the Tunguska region of Siberia leveled 2,000 square miles of forest, laying the trees down flat, their tops pointing away from the epicenter of the explosion. Since there was no crater, scientists have concluded that either a comet or an asteroid composed of rock[4] exploded just above the ground.

According to *Ad Astra*, "If a Tunguska-sized comet hit a typical rural portion of the United States today, as many as 70,000 people would be killed and property damage would exceed $4 billion. An impact in an urban area would kill 300,000 people, with property damage exceeding $280 billion" (32).

Now here's the encouraging news: "There may be several hundred thousand to a few million comets and asteroids boasting diameters greater than 50 meters—the lower end of estimates for the size of the Tunguska comet—that happen to have orbits crossing that of the earth" (Ibid., 34).

Recently, the Hubble Space Telescope enabled astronomers to discover a belt of comets in the vicinity of the planet Pluto. Called the Kuiper Belt, it is "the source of all the comets streaking among the planets with short-period orbits of about twenty years or less" (*The New York Times*, A1). Scientists estimate that the belt, which circles the solar system, could contain as many as ten billion comets ranging from four to two hundred miles in diameter! And beyond the Kuiper Belt scientists speculate that a "shell" of comets surrounds the solar system that is the source of comets such as Halley's comet, which have larger orbits.

Is that "God's arsenal" that Ellen White spoke about in the quotation I shared with you two chapters back? Only He and the angels know when one of these comets might be nudged out of its orbit in the outer reaches of the solar system and race on a trajectory straight toward earth. Should this occur, it would make precious little difference to earth's inhabitants whether God *caused* the event or merely *allowed* it to happen. *First He lets the elements*
I think & here do their job - after the
persecution th' sun, moon, stars

A six-mile asteroid

signs

Scientists have known for years that the skeletal remains *in the*
of dinosaurs can be found in large numbers below a certain *heavens*
point in the geological column, but above that point they *so some*
are totally nonexistent. Because this phenomenon is true in *will still*
the geological column all over the world, they have concluded *repent.*
that the dinosaurs were wiped out all at once. *Then*
Prob. closes
then
punishment
judgements

THE COMING GREAT CALAMITY

Scientists have also wondered for years what caused this sudden death of the dinosaurs. About 1980, Louis Alvarez of the University of California, at Berkeley, proposed an answer: an asteroid impact.[5] Puzzled by the mysterious disappearance of the huge beasts, Alvarez decided to study a black band several inches thick that marks the point in the geological column where the dinosaurs died off. And he found that it contained a concentration of iridium that is significantly higher than what is normally found elsewhere on earth. Asteroids and meteorites, on the other hand, contain a significantly higher concentration of iridium. From this evidence, Alvarez concluded that the dinosaurs were destroyed when a huge asteroid plunged into the earth.

The scientific community scoffed at Alvarez's theory when he first presented it, but within ten years it became the most widely-accepted explanation of the death of the dinosaurs. Since 1980, many scientists have studied the effect that an asteroid impact would have on our planet. And, since the "dinosaur killer" is thought to have been six miles in diameter, a great deal of time has been devoted to investigating the effects of such an asteroid.

Scientists now know that a six-mile asteroid would pack the energy of five billion atomic bombs into a single fireball! As Time-Life's *Comets, Asteroids, and Meteorites* explains it, such an asteroid "would transform cool, blue Earth into a flaming crucible. When the smoke cleared, a transmuted planet would emerge: a hobbled and barren world, reeling toward some new destiny" (121).

And, according to *National Geographic*, "The fireball would have had a radius of several thousand kilometers. Winds of hundreds of kilometers an hour would have swept the planet for hours, drying trees like a giant hair dryer. . . . As much as 90 percent of the world's forest must have burned up" (Ibid.)!

If the asteroid were to hit in the ocean, "an expanding fireball of steam and molten ejecta would level any city within a distance of 1,200 miles and scour the terrain down to bedrock" (*Comets, Asteroids, and Meteorites*, 127). Suddenly, Ellen White's prediction that "thousands of cities will be destroyed" (*Evangelism*, 29) begins to make sense!

A six-mile asteroid plunging into the ocean would also turn the world's seas into a global red tide, and it would kill off most of the world's fish (see *National Geographic*, 681). However, the most devastating result of a six-mile asteroid crashing into the ocean would be tidal waves. Here is how *Newsweek* describes it:

> If the asteroid hit in the Gulf of Mexico, it would have created a wave three miles [16,000 feet] high. Nine hundred miles away, the mammoth wall of water would still be 1,500 feet high. Such an asteroid would cause floods in Kansas City (60).

Let's pause now and look again at what Luke said in quoting Jesus' prediction of signs in the heavens: "There will be signs in the sun, moon, and stars. On the earth, nations will be in anguish and perplexity *at the roaring and tossing of the sea*" (Luke 21:25, emphasis supplied).

You'd think Jesus might have said that the nations would be in anguish and perplexity because of the falling of the stars, but He said that they would be in anguish and perplexity *at the roaring and tossing of the sea*. What relationship, pray tell, could there possibly be between falling stars and the roaring and tossing of the sea? The quotation I shared with you from *Newsweek* answers that question. An asteroid impact in the ocean would indeed cause a "roaring and tossing of the sea," that is, a tidal wave.

THE COMING GREAT CALAMITY

I find it extremely significant that Ellen White endorsed this interpretation of Jesus' words. She begins the quotation below by quoting Luke 21:25 from the King James Version:

> "And there shall be signs in the sun, and in the moon, and in the stars; and upon the earth distress of nations, *the sea and the waves roaring*."

Please pay careful attention to what she says next, especially the words that I have italicized:

> Yes, *they [the sea and the waves] shall pass their borders*, and destruction will be in their track (*Selected Messages*, 3:417, emphasis supplied).

A couple of chapters back, I pointed out that in this statement Ellen White predicted tidal waves as a part of the coming crisis. Now I want to call your attention to the fact that she said that these tidal waves would come as a fulfillment of Jesus' prediction about signs in the sun, moon, and stars! And the quotation from *Newsweek* helps us to understand that an asteroid impact in the ocean would indeed cause "roaring and tossing of the sea."

Let's get back to that six-mile asteroid and what it would do to our planet. The atmosphere would be affected in at least two ways. The first would be acid rain. In the quote that I shared with you earlier from *Newsweek*, we read that "nitrogen and oxygen in the atmosphere combine into nitric acid; any surviving life crawling out of a burrow or cave, gets pelted with a rain as caustic as the acid in a car battery." The Time-Life book *Comets, Asteroids, and Meteorites* puts it this way:

MARVIN MOORE

The toxic rainfall would defoliate any remaining land plants, acidify lakes, and leach normally insoluble, highly poisonous metals from the soils and rocks, depositing them in streams, ponds, and rivers, where they would sicken or kill much of the surviving aquatic life (131).

The second effect on the atmosphere would be darkness:

> Trillions of tons of microfine rock particles and condensed vapor droplets thrown up by the asteroid impact would soar spaceward, reaching stratospheric heights within seconds. . . .
>
> Soot from the [forest] fires mixed with nitrogen oxide smog produced by the initial and subsequent shock waves would combine with the rapidly spreading dust to form a shroud seventeen miles thick. It would envelop the entire planet within twenty-four hours. . . . The surface of the Earth would be locked away in a blackness thirty times more inky than the darkest moonless night (*Comets, Asteroids, and Meteorites,* 131).

This gives us significant insight into Jesus' prediction of signs in the sun, moon, and stars: An asteroid—a falling star—would indeed darken the sun and the moon. Our pioneers thought of the dark day and the falling of the stars as two events separated by more than fifty years. After all, the only possible fulfillment of Jesus' words that they had any knowledge of *happened* more than fifty years apart. But with modern science, we are able to understand what the pioneers could not: that the falling of the stars will *cause* the darkening of the sun and the moon, making them essentially the same event.

Smaller asteroids

Jesus told His disciples, "When these things begin to take place, stand up and lift up your heads, because your redemption is drawing near" (Luke 21:28). Apparently we are to look for these events to happen over a period of time, because Jesus said, "When you *begin* to see these things take place." He also said that at that time we can know that our redemption "is drawing near." While comets, asteroids, and meteorites may fall from the heavens *at* Christ's coming, Luke's words suggest that the signs in the sun, moon, and stars that Jesus predicted will occur *prior* to His coming. I suspect that they will form a part of the final crisis, which will take place over a period of time shortly before Jesus returns.

However, that presents a problem with what we have discussed thus far about asteroids and their effect on our planet. So far, we have considered what would happen should a six-mile asteroid strike the earth. Nearly all of the literature describing the effect of asteroids on our planet that I have read speaks of an asteroid of that size. However, by now it should be obvious to you that should an asteroid that large impact the earth prior to the second coming of Christ, it would wipe out the human race. Yet the Bible makes it clear that many human beings will be alive on the earth to see Jesus come. Thus, if Jesus' prediction of falling stars referred to events during the final crisis, then the "stars" that fall from the sky will have to be much smaller than six miles in diameter.

Recently someone sent me a copy of the September 1991 issue of *Astronomy* magazine, which had an article about asteroids, and it describes the effect of much smaller objects. In the remainder of this chapter, I would like to share what the *Astronomy*[6] article says.

In recent years at least two asteroids have narrowly missed striking our planet. One, in 1989, was between 100 and 400 meters across. According to *Astronomy*, the explosion from this asteroid would have generated the energy of a 1,000 megaton bomb. Describing it in the present tense, the magazine said:

> Hot gas from the vaporized object shoots into the sky and drags more air with it. A shock wave spreads away from the impact and everything within a hundred kilometers is set on fire from the heat of the blast. About 500 kilometers away the temperature is still a scalding 100° C.
>
> The blast travels outward at 35,000 kilometers per hour and levels everything for 250 kilometers. Material from the impact rains down, mostly in the form of molten droplets of rock. A crater about ten times the diameter of the impactor is left behind. Asteroid 1989 FC has wiped out a city the size of New York in an instant (52).

Astronomy says that "nearly 100 Earth-crossing asteroids have been found so far [asteroids with orbits that intersect the orbit of the earth], most of them in the last five years. At least 1,000 are suspected of lurking out there" (ibid.). These asteroids range in size from ten meters to thirty-eight kilometers. Should the thirty-eight kilometer asteroid strike the earth, it would leave nothing alive. However, *Astronomy* says that

> an impact from even a small asteroid might do little more than disrupt the ecosystem for a few

<u>years</u>. Yet such a "minor" event could destroy civilization. Why is this? Because civilization depends on the exploitation of natural resources, including the agricultural resources we rely upon to feed the world's population. If our food supply is totally disrupted, as it would be in the case of an impact winter, crops would die all over the world. The fragile strands of civilization would quickly unravel. Our species, if not driven to extinction, would be decimated, driving survivors to a stone-age existence (53).

Put these words together with what Jesus said:

- There will be signs in the sun, moon, and stars (Luke 21:25).
- Nations will be in anguish and perplexity (ibid.).
- If those days had not been cut short, no one would survive (Matthew 24:22).

Several years ago, when I first began speaking publicly about the possibility that Jesus' prediction about falling stars and dark days possibly referring to comets and asteroids, some people feared that I was being too sensational. However, I never hear that objection anymore. Too many people have heard too much about them on TV and have read too much about them in the newspapers and news magazines.

As recently as May 19, 1996, an asteroid missed planet Earth by a mere 279,000 miles.[7] That's a long way by our reckoning of distances, but in astronomical terms it's a hair's breadth. The asteroid, the largest ever observed passing so close to our planet, was about three-quarters of a mile across. Had it impacted the earth, it would have produced an explosion equivalent to nearly the entire world's nuclear arsenal exploding at one time.

Most significant, perhaps, is the fact that astronomers did not spot the asteroid until four days before it whizzed past the earth. At that late date, had it been on a collision course with our planet, scientists could only have warned the people in the impact area that they were about to die. Only a few of the millions and perhaps billions of doomed people could have been saved. There can be no question that Jesus' prediction would have received a most dramatic fulfillment. The human race would have gone berserk with terror, and the leaders of the world's nations would surely have been in anguish and perplexity, trying to figure out how to handle the horrible catastrophe (Luke 21:25, 26). *Now I know what Jesus meant when He told the women (as He was going to Calvary) to weep for themselves*

Let's take a moment now to bring together all the ideas we have discussed in this chapter and the two that precede it. Ellen White predicted that a final crisis is coming on the earth that will be characterized by calamities "most awful, most unexpected." She said that at least one of these calamities will awaken God's people all over the world. Jesus predicted falling stars, dark days, tidal waves,[8] a terrified human race, and anguish and perplexity among the nations (Luke 21:25, 26). He also predicted a time of distress so severe that it would threaten the survival of the human race (Matthew 24:21, 22).

Adventists have long understood the falling of the stars and the darkening of the sun and the moon to have had a literal fulfillment in past centuries. However, as we have seen, those events do not satisfy Jesus' prediction of a terrified human race as recorded by Luke. I propose to you that if Luke's version of Jesus' words is to be understood literally, then the evidence in this chapter about comets, asteroids, and meteorites is the most satisfactory way to explain what Jesus said.

Before concluding this study about the falling of the stars and their effect, we need to examine some statements Ellen White made about balls of fire. However, since this chapter is already long enough, that will be the subject of our next chapter.

1. Something like this may well have happened in the solar system in past centuries, but until 1994 no one had ever observed such a phenomenon.

2. The comet fragments plunged into Jupiter on the side that faced away from our earth a short time before the spot where they struck the planet came into view. Thus scientists were not able to get a complete view of what happened.

3. I do not accept the 65-million-year chronology, but it is nevertheless true that scientists believe this.

4. There are two kinds of asteroids. Those made from rock tend to explode in the atmosphere, while those made from metal have the density to survive their plunge through the atmosphere and strike the earth.

5. Conservative Christians generally attribute the death of the dinosaurs to the biblical Flood. And a worldwide flood of the magnitude described in the Bible would indeed have killed them all at once. Scientists do not accept the Flood theory. However, the fact that Christians disagree with scientists regarding a worldwide flood is not a reason to question the validity of their conclusions in other areas, one of which is astronomy and asteroids.

6. Since no one has ever experienced a major asteroid impact, most of the data about the effects of asteroid impacts is derived from computer generated models. Thus some discrepancies exist between scientific authorities over the effects of an asteroid impact. In this book I am quoting the authorities I have read. And whatever their differences, all authorities agree that a major asteroid impact would be devastating.

7. *The Idaho Statesman*, May 19, 1996, 11A.

8. Jesus predicted "roaring and tossing of the sea" (Luke 21:25). Ellen White suggested that this meant the sea and the waves "passing their borders"— that is, tidal waves (see *Selected Messages*, 3:417, quoted earlier in this chapter).

CHAPTER SIX

BALLS OF FIRE

At least twice during her lifetime, Ellen White received visions in which she saw balls of fire fall from the sky, and she wrote about these balls of fire on at least four occasions. Because I believe these balls of fire are relevant to our discussion, I would like us to review what she said.

From the available evidence, it is clear that Ellen White received one vision about balls of fire in 1904 and another in 1906. The first two statements below are from her 1904 vision, and the third and fourth are based on the 1906 vision. I will give you the statements first, and then we will analyze them:

Statements reporting on the 1904 vision

Last night a scene was presented before me. I may never feel free to reveal all of it, but I will reveal a little.

It seemed that an immense ball of fire came

down upon the world, and crushed large houses. From place to place rose the cry, "The Lord has come! The Lord has come!" Many were unprepared to meet Him, but a few were saying, "Praise the Lord!"

"Why are you praising the Lord?" inquired those upon whom was coming sudden destruction?"

"Because we now see what we have been looking for."

"If you believed these things were coming, why did you not tell us?" was the terrible response. "We did not know about these things. Why did you leave us in ignorance? Again and again you have seen us; why did you not become acquainted with us, and tell us of the judgment to come, and that we must serve God, lest we perish? Now we are lost!" (Manuscript 102, 2 July 1904, cited in *Reflecting Christ*, 143).

Not long ago a very impressive scene passed before me. I saw an immense ball of fire falling among some beautiful mansions, causing their instant destruction. I heard someone say, "We knew that the judgments of God were coming upon the earth, but we did not know that they would come so soon. Others said, "You knew? Why then did you not tell us? We did not know." On every side I heard such words spoken (*Review and Herald*, 24 November 1904; an almost identical statement is found in *Testimonies for the Church*, 9:28).

Statements reporting on the 1906 vision

Last Friday morning, just before I awoke, a very impressive scene was presented before me. I seemed to awake from sleep but was not in my home. From the windows I could behold a terrible conflagration. Great balls of fire were falling upon houses, and from these balls fiery arrows were flying in every direction. It was impossible to check the fires that were kindled, and many places were being destroyed. The terror of the people was indescribable. After a time I awoke and found myself at home (Letter 278, 27 August 1906, cited in *Evangelism*, 29).

In the night I was, I thought, in a room but not in my own house. I was in a city, where I knew not, and I heard expression after expression. I rose up quickly in my bed, and saw from my window large balls of fire. Jetting out were sparks, in the form of arrows, and buildings were being consumed, and in a very few minutes the entire block of buildings was falling and the screeching and mournful groans came distinctly to my ears. I cried out in my raised position to learn what was happening: Where am I? And where are our family circle? Then I awoke. But I could not tell where I was for I was in another place than home. I said, O Lord, where am I and what shall I do? It was a voice that spoke, "Be not afraid. Nothing shall harm you" (Manuscript 126, 1906, taken from an Ellen White diary entry dated 23, 27 August 1906; cited in *Manuscript Releases*, 11:361).

There can be no question that Ellen White saw two visions of fireballs falling from heaven. Two lines of evidence make this very clear.

THE COMING GREAT CALAMITY

Dating of the documents. The most persuasive evidence that Ellen White received two "balls of fire" visions is in the dating of the documents where she reported them. In the first statement above, Ellen White said, "Last night a scene was presented before me." Since the date on Manuscript 102 that contains this statement is July 2, 1904, we can assume that she received the vision the night of July 1-2. The second statement above has to be quoting from the same vision, since it was reported in the November 24, 1904, issue of the *Review and Herald.*

The third statement, on the other hand, is from her letter 278, which is dated August 27, 1906. This statement begins with the words, "Last Friday morning . . ." This obviously refers to a date in late August 1906 when she again received a "balls of fire" vision. August 27 fell on Monday, so we can assume that she had her vision on Friday, the twenty-fourth.

The fourth statement, a diary entry, is dated both August 23 and 27, 1906. The similarity between the dates of the third and fourth letters leaves no doubt that these two statements are both describing the 1906 vision. This is confirmed by the internal similarity between the two 1906 statements, as we shall see in a moment.[1]

Internal evidence. The differences between the two groups of statements above are significant enough to lead to the conclusion that each group is reporting on a different vision. On the other hand, the two statements within each group are very similar, leading to the conclusion that they are reporting on the same vision. The chart below, considered as a whole, shows the differences between the two groups of statements. The columns show the similarities between the statements within each group:

CHART AS A WHOLE SHOWS THE DIFFERENCES BETWEEN THE 1904 AND 1906 VISIONS	
Similarities between the two 1904 statements	**Similarities between the two 1906 statements**
• One immense ball of fire	• Balls of fire (plural)
• No fiery arrows from the balls of fire	• Fiery arrows from the balls of fire
• God's people say they knew God's judgments were coming	• God's people say nothing
• The wicked reproach God's people for saying nothing	• People are terrified, screeching and groaning

Other issues

What did Ellen White see? Now that we have settled the matter of two visions and which statements report which ones, the larger question presents itself: *What* did Ellen White see? She herself does not say. And for the next forty years after she made these statements, Adventists scratched their heads and wondered what on earth she meant.

Then came 1945, Hiroshima and Nagasaki, and a light went on in Adventist heads. "Why, of course, she was talking about atomic bombs!" we said, and for the next forty-five years that's what most of us understood her to mean. However, from about 1990 to the present, the world has been increasingly aware of the danger to human survival from comets, asteroids, and meteorites. Thus, in recent years many Adventists have begun to ask whether Ellen White's balls of fire may not have been comets or meteorites falling from the sky.

Ellen White says only that she saw balls of fire, and I feel certain that she had no idea what caused them. However, it's obvious that the destruction she describes comes nowhere near to matching either the devastation we read about in the previous chapter about comets and asteroids or the destruction that was caused by the atomic explosions at Hiroshima and Nagasaki. Therefore, if we interpret her fireballs to mean either of these, we must conclude that the atomic weapons or the objects from the sky were comparatively small.

This still does not answer the question of whether she saw the explosion of atomic weapons, heavenly bodies falling on the earth, or something else that we still have no knowledge of. I cannot, of course, comment on "something else." If we today still have no knowledge of what she actually saw, then we are in the same position as Adventists prior to 1945, who could not have commented on the possibility of Ellen White's words referring to atomic explosions.

The two best options we have in the mid-1990s[2] are atomic explosions and comets or meteorites. Does Ellen White say anything in the four statements that would help us to choose between these two options? The answer is Yes. In both 1904 and 1906 Ellen White reports seeing the fireball or fireballs *fall*. In an atomic explosion, the bomb would fall from the sky, but it would not create a fireball during the time it was falling, and once it exploded into a fireball, it would stop falling. (The mushroom cloud would actually go up). However, a *falling fireball* is exactly what one would see in observing a comet or meteorite penetrate earth's atmosphere from outer space.

Furthermore, in the first statement from 1904, Ellen White says that she saw "an immense ball of fire come down *upon the world*." We might say that an atomic bomb came down upon Moscow, Tokyo, or New York City, but we probably would not say that it came down "upon the world." However, it would be very appropriate to say that a comet, asteroid, or meteorite from outer space came down "upon the world." Thus, the very language Ellen White used to describe the falling of the fireball is more appropriate to a comet or meteorite than it is to an atomic explosion.

For these reasons, I believe that at the present time objects from outside our planet are the best explanation of what Ellen White saw. Yet the possibility remains that we still do not know.

Ellen White and Jesus. Another question we need to address is whether in her vision of fireballs falling from the sky God showed Ellen White the fulfillment of Jesus' prediction of falling stars. This is an attractive idea to people who are anxious to know the future—and who of us isn't?

We need to begin by noting that Ellen White herself never suggested such a relationship and probably never thought of it. This should make us cautious about insisting that there is a relationship. However, common details or specifications are one indication of a relationship between ideas that are not linked in more obvious ways, and we can note several similarities between what Jesus predicted and what Ellen White saw:

- Jesus' falling stars and Ellen White's fireballs are both end-time predictions.
- Both predict fiery objects falling from the sky.
- In both cases, the fiery objects could be fulfilled by comets, asteroids, or meteorites.
- Both predict that these falling objects will cause terror among the people.
- Both predict that God's people will rejoice over these signs (see Luke 21:28).

These factors lead me to conclude that it is appropriate to consider the possibility of a relationship between Jesus' statements and Ellen White's.

Prophets and their culture. One Adventist scholar, whose prophetic interpretation I respect, has pointed out that in giving His prophets visions of the future, God does not go beyond what they could comprehend in terms of their own culture. For example, some people claim that the locusts in Revelation 9:3-10 refer to modern helicopters—black ones, of course! My scholar friend would say No, and I have to agree. We can't assume that all prophetic images can be accurately updated to match things that came into existence after the time of the prophecy.

But being cautious of making extensions such as this does not require that we be so cautious as to insist that Ellen White's balls of fire can be explained only in terms of things she was familiar with in her day.

The capability of the military explosives available at her time might indeed have been adequate to meet the specifications of her two visions, including the falling fireballs and the arrows shooting from them.[3] However, to insist that she was describing the exploding military ammunition of her time is tantamount to saying that she herself would have interpreted the balls of fire in that way. But she made no effort in her statements to identify the cause of the balls of fire. She merely reported seeing them, leaving us to guess what they might be. I suggest that she did not know what she was seeing any more than her contemporaries did.

However, you and I today *can* understand comets and asteroids. We *can* also understand that an asteroid slamming into the ocean would cause a tidal wave, easily fulfilling Jesus' prediction of a roaring and tossing sea; and we can understand that comets and meteorites would easily fulfill Ellen White's falling fireballs. Thus I believe it is perfectly appropriate for us to make an educated guess as to what both Jesus and Ellen White meant.

Should we anticipate these signs? Some people may feel that Adventists have no business speculating about such things as future balls of fire. I would point out to such persons that it was God, not I, who gave Ellen White two visions about balls of fire; and it was she, not I, who, on at least four occasions, wrote about balls of fire. I am merely trying to understand what she—and God—meant by these things.

I would also point out that when God's people saw these balls of fire, they said, "Praise the Lord"; and when the people asked why they were praising the Lord, they replied, "Because we now see what we have been looking for."

Far from being too speculative, *Ellen White suggests that God's people ought to be looking for these balls of fire!* God's people are looking for stars falling from heaven.

And where, I would ask, did the people in Ellen White's statements get the idea that they should look for these balls of fire? I can think of at least two sources: Luke's statements, which we examined in the previous chapter, and Ellen White's own "balls of fire" statements, which we have reviewed in this chapter.

Two other statements

Ellen White made two other statements, which, in combination with a statement in the Bible, are relevant to our discussion in this chapter. In *Last Day Events* she said:

> The Lord calls for His people to locate away from the cities, for in such an hour as ye think not, fire and brimstone will be rained from heaven upon these cities (95).

THE COMING GREAT CALAMITY

This sounds a lot like the Bible's description of the destruction of Sodom and Gomorrah:

> Then the Lord rained upon Sodom and Gomorrah brimstone and fire from the Lord out of heaven (Genesis 19:24, KJV).

Now compare this with a statement in the "Ellen G. White Comments" section of volume 5 of the *Seventh-day Adventist Bible Commentary:*

> As the sun arose for the last time upon the cities of the plain, the people thought to commence another day of godless riot. . . . Suddenly as the thunder peal from an unclouded sky, fell balls of fire on the doomed capital (1122).

Then the balls of fire are fire + brimstone like Sodom + Gomorrah.

A simple syllogism should make the logic of these three statements clear. A syllogism consists of two propositions that together lead to a logical conclusion. Following is the syllogism I would like you to consider:

- Proposition 1: Ellen White said that fire and brimstone will fall on the cities in the last days.
- Proposition 2: She described the fire and brimstone that fell on Sodom and Gomorrah as "balls of fire."
- Conclusion: Therefore, balls of fire will fall on the cities in the last days.

The conclusion of a syllogism can be valid only if both propositions are completely valid, and perhaps an expert in logic could poke holes in one or both of my propositions. However, the validity of my conclusion is greatly strengthened by the fact that in several other statements, which we read earlier in this chapter, Ellen White spoke about balls of fire falling upon the cities of the world in the last days.

This concludes our discussion of the nature of the judgments of God that will come upon the world during the final crisis. It is now time to examine the response of the human race to these disasters. We will look first at what Bible prophecy suggests about the human response, and then we will examine what one social scientist has written.

------

1. The dates on the diary entry suggest that Ellen White began her diary entry on the twenty-third, had her vision on the twenty-fourth, and completed the diary entry, including a report of the vision, on the twenty-seventh.

2. I wrote this chapter on July 16, 1995—the fiftieth anniversary of the explosion of the first experimental atomic bomb at White Sands, New Mexico, on July 16, 1945!

3. For example, Francis Scott Key's "The Star Spangled Banner," describing a naval battle in the war of 1812, speaks of "bombs bursting in air," which presumably would have created "fiery arrows" flying from the explosions.

CHAPTER SEVEN

PARADIGM SHIFTS
and Bible Prophecy

In chapter 1, I explained that a paradigm shift is a change in the basic way that humans explain reality. Greek Hellenism, which dominated Western thinking for several hundred years, was the world's best effort at that time to explain reality on a rational basis. However, by Christ's time, the rational explanation of reality was beginning to lose its hold on the human race. We humans are spiritual beings, and two thousand years ago, the spiritual part of human nature wanted more than rationalism. People were beginning to long for their understanding of reality to have a spiritual component as well.

Many mystery cults arose at this time to meet that need. *And God chose this very time to send His Son into the world.* He chose this very time to introduce His new Christian religion. Christianity provided God's true solution to the human spirit's need.

Christianity eventually came to dominate the Western world and its thought patterns. Religion reigned supreme.

Reality was explained largely in terms of faith. Unfortunately, this was an imbalance in the direction of the spiritual explanation of reality.

Another paradigm shift—the Renaissance and the scientific revolution—came in to counteract this imbalance. *And God chose this very time to bring the Protestant reformation to the world.* However, by the middle of the twentieth century, scientism had skewed our way of understanding reality again. Thus it should come as no surprise that we are even now in the beginning stages of a paradigm shift away from scientism and rationalism and toward the religious and spiritual. *And God has again chosen the time of a major paradigm shift to bring a great message to the world*—the final warning just before the second coming of Christ.

It should hardly surprise us that a major paradigm shift will be underway—and indeed will have been completed—at the time that earth's final events take place. Bible prophecy, especially Revelation 13 and 17, makes it clear that the very conditions we now see developing around us are to prevail in the world just before Jesus comes again.

Unfortunately, during most of our history as Seventh-day Adventists, we have had our eyes so fixed on the actual events of the end time that we have failed to notice the backdrop for those events. Yet the background is as clear in the prophecies themselves as the events.

Revelation 13:1-8

Let's begin with Revelation 13:1-4 and verse 8. As you read these verses, especially verse 4, notice that it describes a very spiritual, religious state of society:

> [1]And I saw a beast coming out of the sea. He had ten horns and seven heads, with ten crowns

on his horns, and on each head a blasphemous name. ²The beast I saw resembled a leopard, but had feet like those of a bear and a mouth like that of a lion. The dragon gave the beast his power and his throne and great authority. ³One of the heads of the beast seemed to have had a fatal wound, but the fatal wound had been healed. The whole world was astonished and followed the beast. ⁴Men worshiped the dragon because he had given authority to the beast, and they also worshiped the beast and asked, "Who is like the beast? Who can make war with him?" . . .

⁸All inhabitants of the earth will worship the beast—all whose names have not been written in the book of life belonging to the Lamb that was slain from the creation of the world.

People who are totally committed to secularism are not usually interested in religion, except perhaps as a curious topic for scientific study. But Revelation tells us that the whole world will be amazed at this beast—so amazed that they follow it and worship it. God's own people are the only ones who will refuse to worship this beast. Scientists, university professors, and the leading executives of the world's largest businesses will bow down to this antichristian power. This hardly sounds like the intellectual, rational world that most of us reading this book grew up in!

Had we noticed this detail in Revelation 13 a hundred years ago, we could have predicted that the paradigm shift we are experiencing right now would occur. We would also have known that the events of the end time could not have occurred until the shift took place. Unfortunately, we were too interested in seeing those events happen "now" to read Revelation 13 that carefully.

Revelation 13:11-17

The last half of Revelation 13 paints a picture that is similar in many respects to the first half:

> He [the second beast] was given power to give breath to the image of the first beast, so that it could speak and cause all who refused to worship the image to be killed. He also forced everyone, small and great, rich and poor, free and slave, to receive a mark on his right hand or on his forehead, so that no one could buy or sell unless he had the mark, which is the name of the beast or the number of his name (verses 15-17).

This is enforced religion, which means that the world's governments will be under the control of religious authorities at the end of time. In today's world, about the only political system that is under that degree of religious control is Iran. However, according to Revelation 13, at the very end of time governments all over the world will come under the domination of religious authorities.

Notice, also, that in this passage religion is in control of the world's economic institutions as well. The lamb-like beast commands that anyone who refuses to worship in the politically correct way will be refused the right to buy or sell.

Revelation 17

In some ways, Revelation 17 shows us the dramatic paradigm shift that will occur in the world just before Jesus returns even more explicitly than does chapter 13:

> One of the seven angels who had the seven bowls came and said to me, "Come, I will show you the

punishment of the great prostitute, who sits on many waters. With her the kings of the earth committed adultery and the inhabitants of the earth were intoxicated with the wine of her adulteries."

Then the angel carried me away in the Spirit into a desert. There I saw a woman sitting on a scarlet beast that was covered with blasphemous names and had seven heads and ten horns. The woman was dressed in purple and scarlet, and was glittering with gold, precious stones and pearls. She held a golden cup in her hand, filled with abominable things and the filth of her adulteries. This title was written on her forehead:

MYSTERY
BABYLON THE GREAT
THE MOTHER OF PROSTITUTES
AND OF THE ABOMINATIONS OF THE EARTH.

I saw that the woman was drunk with the blood of the saints, the blood of those who bore testimony to Jesus (verses 1-6).

Two symbols stand out in this prophecy: a woman and a beast. As I am sure you know, in Bible prophecy a beast nearly always represents a nation or political authority, and a woman represents God's people or the church. The pure woman of Revelation 12 represents God's true church, whereas the harlot of Revelation 17 represents the church in deep apostasy.

The first thing to notice about our passage in Revelation 17 is that the woman commits adultery with the kings of the earth. Adultery is a relationship between a man and a woman that God condemns. Thus we can expect that at the very end of time a relationship will develop between the church (the woman) and the governments of the world (the kings) that God condemns.

What will be the nature of this unholy relationship? Verse 3 provides us with the answer. Notice that the woman is riding the beast. This is extremely significant, because a human rider is always in control of the animal it rides. Whether it's a horse, a camel, or an elephant, the human always directs the animal.

A beast in Bible prophecy represents a political entity—a government, and Revelation says that at the very end of time the woman (the Christian Church) will ride the beast (government). An apostate church will be in charge of the world's political systems! This is the adulterous relationship. But it is hardly the arrangement of things in today's secular world! Thus a significant change will have to occur in the relationship between Christianity and the governments of the world before Revelation 17 can be fulfilled.

Revelation goes on to say that the kings of the earth and its inhabitants are intoxicated with the woman's wine. Adventists have always understood wine in Revelation to be a symbol of false doctrine. Thus this verse tells us that all of earth's inhabitants will accept the false teachings of the all-controlling religious power of the end time. Keep in mind that people drink wine for pleasure, albeit a sinful pleasure. These people are not entirely forced into their false spiritual worship. It's sinful, and they enjoy it. They want it. A paradigm shift means that a new way of thinking becomes the way people prefer to view reality. Clearly, in Revelation 17 both the political leaders and the common people (earth's inhabitants) join voluntarily with the woman in thinking her way.

THE COMING GREAT CALAMITY

I cannot emphasize strongly enough that it would have been impossible for Revelation 13 and 17 to be fulfilled in the world of the past couple hundred years.* That world was too rational, too scientific, too secular. It was too uninterested in religious things and often too hostile to religious things. Especially during the twentieth century, secularism has taken complete control of the Western world's major institutions—politics, science, education, communication, etc. Yet it is in the West, especially America, that Adventists have always said these prophecies would find their first fulfillment, and the rest of the world would follow.

Clearly, a major paradigm shift will have been completed when Revelation 13 and 17 reach their fulfillment. Religion will regain the control over the major institutions of society it had during the Middle Ages.

There is, however, a problem we must deal with: Time. Paradigm shifts like those we have been discussing in this chapter take hundreds of years to develop. The most recent paradigm shift, from religion back to rationalism, began in the fifteenth century and did not reach its full maturity until the twentieth century—about five hundred years. Even with our modern methods of communication, a paradigm shift from rationalism back to religious ways of thinking could take one hundred or more years. Are we going to have to wait that much longer for the final events of earth's history?

I believe the answer is No. There is a way for paradigm shifts to occur almost overnight. It's called *crisis*. And crisis is exactly what both the Bible and Ellen White predict will occur in the world shortly before Jesus comes.

In the next chapter we will put crises and paradigm shifts together. We will come up with some interesting conclusions.

78

* Ellen White suggests that Jesus might have returned 100 years ago had God's people been ready. My statement that "it would have been impossible for Revelation 13 and 17 to be fulfilled in the world of the past couple hundred years" does not deny that reality. For the events of the end time to have occurred in the 1890s, the paradigm shift that is going on now would have had to take place 100 years earlier. I'm sure God would have had His ways of bringing that about.

CHAPTER EIGHT

PARADIGM SHIFTS
and Disasters

Several years ago, I happened to be on the campus of Walla Walla College in College Place, Washington, with a couple of extra hours before my next appointment. Not wanting to waste the time, I wandered over to the library. I had been studying the millennium for several weeks, so I decided to see what books the library might have on that subject.

I looked through the library's computerized listing of book titles and came up with several that seemed helpful. I could tell from the catalog numbers on the books that most of them were in the same general vicinity in the stacks. A few minutes later, I found the right shelf and began looking for my books. And, as I often do, I checked that entire section of books to see whether there might be something on the millennium that my computer search had failed to turn up. One book in particular caught my attention: *Disaster and the Millennium* by Michael Barkun.[*]

Mr. Barkun is a social scientist, and thus he writes about the effect that disasters have on individuals and on society as a whole. He proposes that disasters create the circumstances under which paradigm shifts can occur very rapidly. He says, for example, that "disaster creates conditions peculiarly fitted to the rapid alteration of belief systems" (*Disaster and the Millennium*, 113) A belief system is the same thing as the paradigms we have been discussing in this book. Thus we can alter Mr. Barkun's statement to say that "disaster creates conditions peculiarly fitted to rapid paradigm shifts." Notice also the following statements, which say the same thing:

Disaster produces the questioning, the anxiety, and the suggestibility that are required [for change]; only in its wake are people moved to abandon old values of the past (ibid., 6).

Disaster, by removing the familiar environment, removes precisely those frames of reference by which we normally evaluate statements, ideas, and beliefs. Belief systems which under nondisaster conditions might be dismissed, now receive sympathetic consideration (ibid., 56).

Disasters offer unusual natural circumstances for the sudden adoption of new beliefs.
A disaster population suffers a temporary sense of incapacity, vulnerability, and confusion. The collapsed social structure renders traditional authority relationships less effective and traditional statuses less meaningful.
The disaster victim, for whom the ordinary cues and landmarks of living have been removed, is left

passive, receptive to suggestion, and in need of a substitute environment. He requires a new configuration of social relationships and values to explain his new predicament (ibid., 55, 56).

Please notice that the end-time disasters predicted by Jesus and Ellen White will create the perfect climate for human beings to be seeking "new social relationships and values." Or, to put it another way, these disasters will create the perfect psychological environment for a world-wide paradigm shift to occur. Let's look again at the words of Jesus:

> There will be signs in the sun, moon and stars. On the earth, nations will be in anguish and perplexity at the roaring and tossing of the sea. Men will faint from terror, apprehensive of what is coming on the world, for the heavenly bodies will be shaken (Luke 21:25, 26).

> For then there will be great distress, unequaled from the beginning of the world until now—and never to be equaled again. If those days had not been cut short, no one would survive (Matthew 24:21, 22).

In this book we have examined the possibility that exists for natural disasters to occur on a scale unknown to the world since the Flood. We have seen that the prophecies of both the Bible and Ellen White anticipate catastrophes of this magnitude shortly before Jesus returns to earth. I predict that as a result of these disasters, the entire world will become very religious. Religious explanations of reality will once again be preferred by society as a whole.

I also predict that as a result of this paradigm shift, the world's major institutions—government and politics, science, education, entertainment, and the news media—will come under the control of religion. These institutions will once again operate out of religious assumptions about reality.

I predict that this paradigm shift will happen very quickly. I am reminded again of Paul's statement that "when they shall say, Peace and safety; then sudden destruction cometh upon them" (1 Thessalonians 5:3, KJV). And I am reminded of Ellen White's statement that "a sudden, unlooked-for calamity will show whether there is any real faith in the promises of God" (*Christ's Object Lessons*, 412). *Here*

---

* Michael Barkun, *Disasters and the Millennium* (New Haven, Conn.: Yale University Press, 1974).

CHAPTER NINE

DISASTERS
and Millenarian Movements

Perhaps you are wondering why Michael Barkun titles his book *Disasters and the Millennium*. What do disasters have to do with the millennium? If by *millennium* we mean the 1,000 years that will follow the second coming of Christ, not much. However, disasters have everything to do with *millenarian movements*.

Social scientists use the expression *millenarian movement* to refer to a phenomenon that tends to occur any time a large number of religious people get excited thinking about the end of the world. Often these people will make specific predictions about a coming time of natural disasters followed by a time of peace and righteousness. This eschatological excitement is not the millenarian movement; it is the atmosphere in which millenarian movements tend to spring up. Following are the characteristics of millenarian movements as Michael Barkun describes them:[1]

MARVIN MOORE

Characteristics of a Millenarian Movement[2]

- Millenarians believe that salvation is imminent.
- They expect that in the near future the present social order will be completely destroyed and a perfect society will be established.
- They believe their efforts will hasten the destruction of the old order and the establishment of the new.
- They claim to have total truth.
- Millenarians have a belief system that explains life's ultimate questions.
- They demand total commitment to their cause, to the point of abandoning normal activities such as jobs, planting, harvesting, etc. They will sell their property to further "the cause."
- They claim to be a "remnant"—a small group of righteous people in a world that is totally evil.

Do these ideas sound familiar to you? They should. They are a perfect expression of what Seventh-day Adventists believe about themselves. *We are a millenarian movement!* William Miller's preaching created a powerful millenarian movement, and we arose out of that. To this day, Seventh-day Adventists are a millenarian movement.

But what do disasters have to do with millenarian movements? Please notice what Barkun says:

> Millenarian movements almost always occur in times of upheaval, in the wake of culture contact, economic dislocation, revolution, war, and natural catastrophe (45).

> A disaster population suffers a temporary sense of incapacity, vulnerability, and confusion. The

collapsed social structure renders traditional authority relationships less effective and traditional statuses less meaningful. *Under such conditions, millenarian movements appear* (ibid., 55,emphasis supplied).

Barkun's explanation of why disasters tend to create millenarian movements should be easy enough for Seventh-day Adventists to understand:

Often disasters are taken to represent God's punishment, and "the idea of punishment seems strong among certain religious groups who see disasters as indications of apocalyptic changes and millennialist hope"[3] (ibid., 80).[4]

Multiple disasters

Barkun also points out that multiple disasters are much more effective than a single disaster in creating millenarian movements. "One major disaster situation," he says, "does not appear capable of generating . . . millenarianism" (ibid., 78). "Single disasters . . . rarely produce millenarianism" (ibid.).

Why is this true? Millenarian movements occur when a large number of people give up their old belief system and adopt a new one. And, as we learned in the previous chapter, people generally will not do this in a time of peace. But old belief systems are nearly always called into question in a time of disaster, *and multiple disasters are much more effective at doing this than a single disaster.* Notice what Barkun says:

A single disaster is less likely to call existing modes of explanation into serious question, even though the disaster itself may be inexplicable in current cultural terms. . . . All belief systems tend to be preserved as long as possible, even when alternative systems might yield a better understanding. . . .

As disasters and their consequences multiply, however, the inadequacies of traditional modes of explanation become patently obvious (ibid., 79).

Barkun's conclusion that multiple disasters are especially likely to create paradigm shifts and millenarian movements reminds me of Ellen White's comment that "these destructions will follow one after another" (*Evangelism*, 27) and "there will be a *series of events* revealing that God is master of the situation" (*Testimonies for the Church*, 9:96, emphasis supplied). Jesus also suggested that the disasters of the end time will be multiple. He predicted "signs" (plural) in the sun, moon, and stars (Luke 21:25).

Ideological "raw material"

You may be wondering why God bothered to raise up the Seventh-day Adventist Church in the mid-1800s. Why take one hundred and fifty years to do what the disasters of the end time could accomplish in just a few years?

That's a good question, and there's a good answer: Even under the powerful influence of earth's end-time natural disasters, we couldn't do the job in just a few years without the background of the previous one hundred and fifty years. Let me share a quote from Mr. Barkun's book, and then I will explain it:

If multiple disasters represent one typical condition for the rise of millenarian movements, another and essential one is the presence of ideological "raw material." *Ideas must already be present that, without too much distortion, can be interpreted in a salvationist manner* (Barkun, 84, 85, emphasis supplied).

When Barkun says that ideological raw material must already be present at the time of the disaster, he means that the basic ideas people will then champion do not arise out of thin air at the time of the disaster. They must already be present in the society. The disaster merely gives impetus to those ideas that are in place at the time it occurs.

Recognizing this helps us to better understand the mission of the Adventist Church these one hundred and fifty years since 1844. We have not succeeded in winning more than a tiny percentage of the world's population to our message during this time. But perhaps God's larger plan didn't require that we should. What He intended, and what to a great extent we have done, is to plant our unique views all over the world. When the disasters of the end time occur, our ideological raw material will be in place to explain to people everywhere what is going on around them.

So if you feel frustrated right now that the world is not accepting our message the way we could wish, don't get discouraged. Don't give up. The time is coming when our message will be the most logical explanation of what is going on. I would like to share with you the Christmas-tree-light illustration from my book *The Crisis of the End Time*:

Have you ever strung lights on a Christmas tree? First you plug several strings together and wind them in and out among the branches. When the tree is covered with lights, you flip the wall switch and darken the whole room. Then you plug the Christmas-tree lights into a socket in the wall. Instantly every one of those lights flashes on, and the tree is covered with tiny pinpoints of light.

For 150 years Seventh-day Adventists have been "stringing lights" all over the world, and all the while it has seemed as though we were accomplishing so very little. But when the latter-rain power of the Holy Spirit energizes God's church, [and when the disasters of the end time open people's minds to accept the truth], suddenly pinpoints of light will flash on all over the world, and these little lights will rapidly increase until the world is flooded with light (201).

Are you familiar with Global Mission? It's the name of the Seventh-day Adventist Church's most important worldwide evangelism effort of the 1990s. The purpose of Global Mission is to establish an Adventist presence in as many unreached people groups of one million or more as possible by the year 2000.

I can't think of anything that would better fulfill God's purpose for this church at the present time.

While we want to reach as many people as possible, God is not discouraged with us, nor have we failed in our mission, if we do not reach every human being. More important than reaching every human being is planting our ideological raw material in as many places around the world as possible, so that it will "be there" when the disasters of the end time open people's minds to receive it.

I urge you not to give up on the work of this church just because it seems to be accomplishing so little. Continue to support it with all the energy and all the dollars you can spare. You will be helping to put in place the ideological raw material for the time in the near future when the world will need it most.

ADDITIONAL NOTE

Barkun's conclusion that millenarian movements especially tend to appear in times of disaster poses an interesting question for Seventh-day Adventists. No major natural disasters or military upheavals were occurring in the 1830s and 1840s when William Miller's millenarian movement occurred. And while our church has lived through two world wars, our movement was not *created* by those world wars. Thus, if disasters tend to create millenarian movements, how did we become a millenarian movement without the presence of disasters in the society in which we sprang up? Barkun answers that question. While he does not mention either William Miller or Seventh-day Adventists in the following quotation, he speaks of the very time and place in which our movement sprang up:

> There are, to be sure, exceptions [times when millenarian movements arise apart from disaster]. Upstate New York was relatively tranquil during the period 1825-60, yet was so often swept by millenarian fervor that it came to be known as the "Burned-Over District." For the vast majority of cases, however, some instability in the environment seems to call the [millenarian] movement into existence (Barkun, 45).

In doing this study I have often asked myself, Why was the Millerite precursor to Adventism an exception to the general rule that millenarian movements arise out of disaster? Why did God raise us up as a millenarian movement between 1830 and 1860—a time of relative peace?

The answer is quite simple. God knew that disasters don't create ideological raw material. They only appropriate it. Thus, logically, the ideological raw material around which His end-time millenarian movement will unite had to be put in place prior to the disasters, during a time of peace.

I believe God also knew that it would take at least one hundred and fifty years for His people to spread that ideological raw material all over the world and that this task would be next to impossible to accomplish under the difficult circumstances that disasters create. He foresaw that we would need one hundred and fifty years of relative peace to accomplish our mission. Thus He arranged for our movement to arise during a time of relative peace. If disaster creates the circumstances out of which millenarian movements generally arise, then I suggest that divine providence was the primary factor making us an exception to that rule. Barkun simply was not in a position to understand that. All he could do was point out the exception. He could not state the reason for it.

---

1. Michael Barkun, *Disaster and the Millennium* (New Haven, Conn.:Yale University Press, 1974). See chapter 8 for a statement about who Michael Barkun is.
2. This list is not a direct quote from Mr. Barkun's book. He mentions various characteristics of millenarian movements throughout his book. I brought these characteristics together here.
3. Barkun apparently quotes an authority in this statement, because a portion of it is in quotation marks. However, he does not give a reference.
4. See Additional Note at the end of this chapter for a discussion of why Seventh-day Adventists became a millenarian movement without the influence of natural disasters or war.

CHAPTER TEN

A MODERN DECEPTION

On May 13, 1917, three children—Francisco Marto (age 9), Jacinta Marto (his sister, aged 7), and Lucia Santos (aged 10)—were tending sheep near the Portuguese village of Fatima at a place called the Cova da Iria (Cove of Irene). Suddenly they saw a flash of lightning, and a moment later a beautiful young woman appeared over a nearby oak tree. "Do not be afraid," she said. "I will not harm you. I am from heaven."[1]

Lucia asked the lady what she wanted. "I want you to come to this place at this same time on the thirteenth day of the month for the next six months," the lady replied. "Then I will tell you who I am and what I want." She also asked them if they would be willing to offer themselves to God "to endure all the sufferings which He may wish to send you in reparation for the countless sins by which He is offended, and in supplication for the conversion of sinners."

Lucia said they would be willing to do that.

"Then you will have much to suffer," the lady said, "but the grace of God will be your comfort." The children then saw rays of light beaming from her open hands. She concluded her visit by admonishing the children to "say the rosary every day to earn peace for the world and the end of the war [World War I]." Then she disappeared.

When the children reported what they had seen, their parents and others scoffed. However, a month later they allowed the children to return to the Cova da Iria, and a few curious adults went with them. After about fifteen minutes, Lucia pointed to the sky. "There comes the lady!" she exclaimed. The adults watched as the branches of the oak tree bent down, even though no human hands were touching them. By the time the encounter was over, the adults were convinced that the children had spoken to the Virgin Mary, and they reported the event far and wide. Word spread rapidly throughout the region.

Some 5,000 people showed up at the Cova da Iria to watch the children talk to the lady on July 13. This time she told the children a secret and gave them strict instructions not to divulge it to anyone. She also promised that on October 13 she would perform a miracle "so that everyone may see and believe." She held out her hands, and light streamed from them. Lucia said the light penetrated the earth, and she saw a vision of hell. "You have seen hell where the souls of poor sinners go," the lady said. "To save them God wants to establish devotion to my immaculate heart throughout the world."

Now the story of the children's encounter with "the Virgin Mary" spread like wildfire. Even the newspapers reported the event, though with great derision. One newspaper accused the Jesuits of concocting the story as a way to gain political power!

THE COMING GREAT CALAMITY

On August 13, 15,000 people showed up at the Cova da Iria, but the children were not there. They had been kidnapped a few moments earlier by the local Communist magistrate,[2] who was anxious to prove the whole story a hoax. However, the people saw a globe of light move across the sky from the east and settle on the oak tree. Six days later, on the nineteenth, the lady appeared to the children and repeated her promise to perform a miracle on October 13 "so that all may believe in my apparitions."

By September 13 enthusiasm was running so high that thirty thousand people showed up! These also saw the globe of light settle over the oak tree, and they saw bright petals falling through the air like snow. And the lady repeated her promise of a miracle on October 13.

The rain was coming down in torrents the morning of October 13, but then the sky suddenly cleared. Upward of seventy-five thousand people[3] turned out to see "the miracle." They were not disappointed. The children saw "the lady" again, and as she was leaving, she opened her hands, and this time, rays of light beamed toward the sun. As the people watched, the sun grew pale, like a silver disk in the sky. Rays of many colors shone from the sun in every direction: red, blue, yellow, green—all the colors of the light spectrum. Suddenly the sun turned into a giant wheel of fire spinning madly on its axis. It danced wildly in the sky, and then it appeared to break loose from its orbit and fall toward the earth. It turned blue and then yellow. Soon yellow spots began falling all over the landscape.

One of the newspapers reported that "the people . . . gazed at the sun which trembled and made brusque and un-heard of movements beyond all cosmic laws. The sun seemed literally to dance in the sky."[4]

Following this supernatural display, the sun returned

to its place in the sky, the rain stopped, and the clouds disappeared. And the people, who had been drenched to the skin by the rain, noticed that their clothes were completely dry. Not only that, the ground was completely dry where just fifteen minutes earlier water had been standing in pools up to three inches deep!

Fatima is without a doubt the best known Marian apparition in modern times, but it is by no means the only one. Many people claim to have seen the virgin. Indeed, in the last fifteen or twenty years, people in nearly every country of the world claim to have seen either the Virgin Mary herself or statues of the virgin sweating blood and weeping tears. A document I have in my files titled *Queen of Peace*[5] lists several dozen such appearances since 1970. Countries where these apparitions have been seen include France, Nicaragua, Ukraine, Korea, United States, Canada, and Italy, to name a few.

Among the many Marian apparitions of the last 150 years, several have taken on a certain fame. The first of these occurred in 1846, when two children in the French village of LaSalette claimed to have seen the Virgin Mary. Fatima occurred in 1917, followed by an apparition on July 2, 1961, to four young girls in the Spanish village of Garabandal. More recently, a group of nuns in Akita, Japan, claim to have received visions of the virgin, and a Father Don Stefano Gobbi, also of Akita, claims to have received "locutions" (oral messages) from her.

The most famous apparitions during the latter half of the twentieth century have occurred in Medjugorje, a small town in Bosnia. The Medjugorje visions have also been the spark for apparitions in many other parts of the world, including a number in the United States.[6]

The Medjugorje visions began on June 24, 1981, when five teenagers claimed to have seen the virgin as they were walking along a road at the foot of Mount Podbrdo. A sixth young person was with them when they saw a similar vision the next day. In each of the other instances of Marian apparitions cited in this chapter, the visions ceased after a time. However, the young people in Medjugorje claim to have received visions regularly from 1981 right up to the present time (January 1996). Medjugorje has also become a very popular site for pilgrimages. Tens of thousands of people flock there each year, and the war in that part of the world between 1993 and 1995 did little to stop them.

The question naturally arises, What does this all mean? Perhaps the first thing we should consider is what Catholics themselves think of these apparitions.

The church makes a careful inquiry into each report of an apparition of the virgin. An investigation typically begins with the local bishop. If he has reason to believe that the reported apparition is credible, he will pass the incident on to higher levels of the church for continued investigation. Once the church pronounces an apparition to be miraculous, a shrine is usually built over the spot where it occurred, and the faithful are admonished to take pilgrimages to these shrines.

However, the church is very cautious about what it will proclaim to be a miraculous apparition. Only about half a dozen such occurrences have been certified by the church in recent times. When careful investigation fails to provide sufficient evidence to certify that an apparition really did occur, Catholic leaders usually advise their members not to take pilgrimages to the shrine or to give it any other special attention. (Humanity being what it is, though, the faithful often do not pay attention to these admonitions from the hierarchy.)

The next question is, What should Seventh-day Adventists think of these apparitions?

It would be easy to dismiss them all as tabloid sensationalism, something on the order of the predictions that psychics make at the beginning of each year. I do not doubt for a moment that some so-called apparitions of the Virgin Mary are the result of people "seeing things." I'm not too impressed when someone claims to have seen the face of Jesus in the clouds, the Virgin Mary in the grain on a wooden door, or the archangel Michael in the reflection off the surface of a shiny car.

However, neither must we dismiss all claims of Marian apparitions as the foolishness of gullible people. The children at Fatima did predict several months in advance that a miracle would occur on October 13, 1917, and seventy-five thousand people saw it happen. Indeed, two secular newspapers, which had derided the children's story up to that point, reported the events of October 13 in great detail. Thus it really is not possible to brush off the events at Fatima as a fraud. We *must* take them seriously. Something supernatural—something miraculous—has happened, at least in some of the better-known apparitions, and probably in some of those of lesser fame as well.

And here is where Seventh-day Adventists need to be cautious, for Scripture makes it very clear that false miracles will be one of the major deceptions of Satan in the end time. Jesus said that "false Christs and false prophets will appear and perform great signs and miracles to deceive even the elect—if that were possible" (Matthew 24:24). Paul predicted that "the coming of the lawless one will be in accordance with the work of Satan displayed in all kinds of counterfeit miracles, signs, and wonders, and in every sort of evil that deceives those who are perishing" (2 Thessalonians 2:9, 10). And according to John, writing in Revelation, the second beast of chapter 13 will deceive the inhabitants of the earth with "great and miraculous signs" (verses 13, 14).

Thus it was with good reason that Ellen White advised us to test every miracle by the testimony of Scripture.[7] Please follow through with me as we do that.

I have already mentioned a couple of points that should alert any Seventh-day Adventist who is familiar with the Bible to be cautious. Catholics are absolutely certain that the Virgin Mary has been in heaven since she died some 2,000 years ago. However, the Bible teaches that when human beings die they remain unconscious in their graves. Thus Mary has not been in heaven for 2,000 years, nor is it she who is communicating with the visionaries in these so-called Marian apparitions. Neither are any of the miracles associated with these apparitions from God.

Lucia, one of the visionaries at Fatima, claimed that on July 13 God gave her a vision of hell, where she saw sinners suffering in the flames. But the Bible teaches that hell will not burn until after the millennium (see Revelation 20:14, 15). It is not burning now, and sinners are not being sent there now. The wicked as well as the righteous remain in the grave until the resurrection. Thus any vision that claims to show people "the reality of hell" is not from God.

Catholics teach that sinners who are not quite good enough for heaven but not bad enough for hell go to an intermediate place called purgatory, where the process of purification from sin continues. Eventually, the sinners in purgatory are supposed to be able to make it to heaven through their own efforts and the many prayers and Masses said on their behalf by their loved ones still living on earth. However, this is a pure fabrication of the Catholic Church. The doctrine of purgatory has no support whatsoever in the Bible. Yet the Virgin Mary has told several of the visionaries to "pray for the souls in purgatory."[8] I do not hesitate to say that *God does not support such teachings in any of His legitimate communications with the human race.*

False teachings about life after death lay the foundation for spiritualism, as every Seventh-day Adventist knows. And spiritualistic manifestations have been a part of some Marian apparitions. On one occasion, the visionaries at Garabandal, Spain, claimed to have conversed with a Father Luis Andreu, the dead brother of a Father Ramon Andreu. Here is the visionaries' report of this conversation:

> A few days after Father Luis' death, the Blessed Virgin told us that we were going to talk to him. . . . At eight or nine o'clock in the evening, the Blessed Virgin appeared to us smiling, very, very much, as usual. She said to the four of us: "Father Luis will come now and speak with you." A moment later, he came and called us one by one. We didn't see him at all but only heard his voice. It was exactly like the one he had on earth. When he had spoken for a while, giving us advice, he told us certain things for his brother, Father Ramon Maria Andreu.[9]

"Confirmation" that Father Luis himself had talked to the visionaries came when they told Father Ramon what his brother had said: "Father Ramon was told precise details of his brother's funeral and details of his personal life that were unknown to anyone but himself."[10] This is spiritualism in its most beautiful yet most blatant form!

I have also found a heavy emphasis on righteousness by works in the Catholic literature I have read about apparitions of the Virgin Mary. Mary constantly advises the visionaries to reform their lives, stop sinning, do penance, say the rosary, and carry out all manner of rites and rituals. In all the hundreds of pages I have read in these books and magazine articles, not once have I found a clear teaching about salvation by grace alone through faith. It is all works, works, works.

One of the most distressing themes that occurs over and over in this Marian literature is the idea that human beings on earth today are to make reparation for sinners. To make reparation in this sense means to make amends, to make up for a wrong or injury, to make compensation.[11] That, of course, is what Jesus did on the cross. No other human is worthy to make reparation for sinners, and it is blasphemous to suppose that Christ asks them to do so. Yet one of the most frequent messages the visionaries report receiving from Mary is that God is angry with the world because of its many sins; Jesus' heart is very sad; and by their many sacrifices, the visionaries can avert God's anger and make Jesus happy.

"Pray a great deal and make sacrifices for sinners," one visionary was told, "for many souls go to hell for not having someone to pray and make sacrifices for them."[12] Apparently Christ's sacrifice on the cross was inadequate to save sinners from hell! And this is typical of countless statements in the Marian literature I have read. Even little children are made responsible for keeping God and Jesus happy! One Catholic author had this to say about the children who received the vision at Fatima:

> After the miracle of the sun, the three children continued their long prayers and formidable penances, regardless of health considerations. Eventually a holy and sympathetic priest, Fr. Faustino, persuaded them to modify their excesses

within the bounds of prudence. All the same, Francisco would spend long hours daily before the tabernacle "consoling the hidden Jesus" as he would say to his companions, while Jacinta would kneel in tears for hours on end, imploring God to save souls from the terrifying inferno of Hell. One day, Francisco went missing. There was a long, anxious search for him. Finally, Lucia found him lying face down behind a wall in the fields, as if in a trance. "Francisco!" she called, shaking him anxiously. "What are you doing?" The little boy gradually roused himself and with a far-away gaze murmured, "I've been thinking of God. I've been thinking of all the sins which make Him so sad. If only I could console Him."

I protest! That's spiritual child abuse! God is perfectly capable of taking care of His own emotions. While He surely rejoices over every sinner who repents (see Luke 15:7), I don't believe He makes humans responsible for His happiness, and He certainly lays no such burden on eight- and ten-year-old children!

But the most blasphemous teaching, which shows up over and over in these apparitions of the so-called Virgin Mary, is that she is a co-redeemer and a co-mediator with Jesus. One Catholic author, who is typical of many, wrote:

Since our salvation has been wrought in this [Mary's] Heart and through this Heart, it is evident that after God and His Son Jesus, this is the first foundation from which we cannot separate ourselves without incurring the evident danger of ruin and eternal damnation. . . .

THE COMING GREAT CALAMITY

> There is also consecration, first of all to the most Sacred Heart of Jesus, Man and God, and then to the Immaculate Heart of Mary, united with Jesus in the work of salvation. . . .
>
> Therefore, the charity of Mary suffering with Christ . . . lies at the source of her expiatory and coredemptrix action.[13]

The examples I have listed of the false doctrines taught by the so-called Virgin Mary should be enough to persuade anyone who has even a partial understanding of biblical truth[14] that these apparitions are *not* from God. Thus the conclusion is inescapable that since at least some of them are clearly supernatural, they have to be from Satan.

I know that what I just said sounds terribly harsh and judgmental, perhaps even bigoted to some people. However, we are living in the very final days of earth's history; the forces of evil are rapidly building up for the final conflict; and I must warn God's people that a terrible deception awaits them, which will sweep nearly the entire world into its ranks.

The conclusions I have shared with you in this chapter regarding Marian apparitions are reinforced by authors Elliot Miller and Kenneth R. Samples in their book *The Cult of the Virgin: Catholic Mariology and the Apparitions of Mary*.[15] At the time they wrote their book, Miller and Samples were researchers with the Christian Research Institute in San Juan Capistrano, California—a cult watchdog organization established by cult-expert Walter R. Martin.

In the first half of the book, Miller gives a careful Protestant evaluation of the Catholic view of Mary; Samples evaluates Marian apparitions in the second half of the book. Following are some of Samples's conclusions:

Because Catholic Mariology and Marian apparitions are inextricably woven together (Mariology provides the basis for potentially authentic apparitions), we must jettison both. If we are forced to reject the Catholic view of Mary on scriptural grounds [which Miller, in the first half of the book, concludes Protestants must do], we cannot then accept Marian apparitions that simply espouse the same doctrinal errors. We Protestants, therefore, have a scriptural right to discount Marian apparitions a priori, simply because they fail our criterion (ibid., 128).

Samples does not stop with rejecting the Marian apparitions as false, however. He continues with the crucial task of evaluating their origin:

Any honest effort to provide a satisfying explanation for the phenomenon known as Marian apparitions will prove to be a complex and difficult task. *I freely admit that I may not be able to account for everything connected to these unusual occurrences. Nevertheless, logically the origin or cause of Marian apparitions must be either natural or supernatural.* . . . Because of the unbiblical nature of Marian apparitions, if the cause is supernatural in origin then we can only be dealing with the demonic, not with God. I realize that this line of reasoning will be offensive to many Catholics; nonetheless, I believe it is a necessary theological inference (ibid., 129, emphasis supplied).

THE COMING GREAT CALAMITY

In the course of writing his book, Samples spent time in Medjugorje. He talked with the six young people who claim to have received visions of the Virgin Mary, and he also talked to both their supporters and their critics in Bosnia. He said that, contrary to those who claimed the young people were mentally unbalanced, he found them to be quite emotionally stable and believable. "They appear to be normal young adults," he said, "certainly not psychologically unbalanced." He also pointed out that there has also been some "good fruit," as he calls it, as a result of the Marian apparitions in Medjugorje (ibid., 131). He adds, however, that while

> the visionaries' believability adds credence to a *supernatural* explanation for the events, . . . it does not assure us that this supernatural source is of God. It is possible for well-adjusted people to be *sincerely* deceived. And if the apparitions are demonic in origin, then their good fruit is nothing more than an enticing delusion (ibid., emphasis supplied).

One other aspect of Samples's research struck me as extremely significant. I will let Samples tell you the story, and I think you will immediately recognize its significance:

> Another troubling aspect of Medjugorje is that some of the visionaries have seen, talked to, and even touched people who have died. In Ivanka's case, she embraced and kissed her dead mother on several occasions. During an interview, Ivanka described these encounters with her mother: "I've seen my mother three times since she died! . . . My favorite time was the last time she was with the Blessed

Mother. My mother came over to me. She put her arms around me and kissed me. She said, 'Oh, Ivanka, I am so proud of you' " (ibid., 132, 133).

Please note Samples's conclusion, which is identical to what Seventh-day Adventists would conclude: "This sounds very similar to the occultic practice of necromancy [talking to the dead], a practice that the Bible explicitly condemns (Deut. 18:10-12; Isa. 8:19; 1 Chron. 10:13-14)" (ibid., 133).

I used to wonder how Satan was going to bring the whole world under the influence of spiritualism, when most conservative Protestants and many conservative Catholics are very aware of the dangers of New Age spiritualism. I believe that one of the most significant ways in which he will do this is through these so-called apparitions of the Virgin Mary. What, after all, could be more heart-warming and comforting than for the mother of Jesus to communicate with the human race with messages from Him! And how could anyone dare to oppose such a wonderful "truth"!

In this light, the following statement by Ellen White takes on new meaning:

> As the spirits will profess faith in the Bible, and manifest respect for the institutions of the church, their work will be accepted as a manifestation of divine power. . . .
>
> Papists, who boast of miracles as a certain sign of the true church, will be readily deceived by this wonder-working power; and Protestants, having cast away the shield of truth, will also be deluded.[16]

It is true, as I pointed out earlier, that the Catholic Church is very cautious about what it certifies as a ine miracle. However, once the church confirms that a Marian apparition is genuinely supernatural, then all Catholics are urged to accept the messages from that apparition as from God. But if these apparitions are all a deception of Satan, then it doesn't matter whether a person believes one of them or all of them. He or she will be deceived.

Perhaps you are wondering what all of this has to do with disasters, calamities, and the judgments of God, which are the theme of this book.

It has everything to do with them.

Please keep reading.

---

1. Many accounts of the events at Fatima in 1917 have been written in the English language. The English wording of the many statements by "Mary" and the children varies slightly from one account to another, primarily due, I suspect, to differences in translation. Thus I have not given any references for these quotations.
2. Portugal was under Communist domination at this time.
3. No one knows how many people showed up on October 13. I have read estimates ranging from fifty thousand to one hundred thousand.
4. Cited by John M. Haffert in *Russia Will Be Converted* (Washington, N.J.: AMI Press, 1950), 63.
5. Published by the Pittsburgh Center for Peace, 6111 Steubenville Pike, McKees Rocks, Penn. 15136.
6. Claims of U.S. apparitions have been made in Scottsdale and Phoenix, Arizona; Conyers, Georgia; Denver, Colorado; and Marlboro, New Jersey; to name just a few.
7. See *The Great Controversy*, 593.
8. Ted and Maureen Flynn, *The Thunder of Justice* (Sterling, Va.: Maxkol Communications, 1993), 201, 202.
9. Ibid., 166, 167.
10. Ibid., 167.
11. See *Webster's New World Dictionary*, Second College Edition.
12. *The Thunder of Justice*, 182.
13. Francis Johnson, *Fatima: The Great Sign* (AMI Press, Washington, N.J.: 1980), 115, 116.
14. Many Protestants disagree with Adventists regarding the state of the dead, but they can be well protected against these false Marian apparitions if they will evaluate them in light of the biblical teaching that Jesus Christ is our only

Redeemer and Saviour, and salvation comes by grace alone through faith in His sacrifice for the sins of the world.

15. Elliot Miller and Kenneth R. Samples, *The Cult of the Virgin: Catholic Mariology and the Apparitions of Mary* (Grand Rapids, Mich.: Baker Book House, 1992).

16. *The Great Controversy*, 588.

CHAPTER ELEVEN

A DIFFERENT VIEW
of the end time

If men do not repent and better themselves, the Father will inflict a terrible punishment on all of humanity. It will be a punishment greater than the Deluge [the Flood of Noah], such as one will never have seen before. Fire will fall from the sky and will wipe out a great part of humanity, the good as well as the bad, sparing neither priests nor faithful. The survivors will find themselves so desolate that they will envy the dead.[1]

Sister Agnes Sasagawa of Akita, Japan, said that the Virgin Mary gave her this message on October 13, 1973. Father Don Stefano Gobbi, also of Akita, conveyed a similar message on September 15, 1987:

A chastisement worse than the flood is about to come upon this poor and perverted humanity. Fire

108

will descend from Heaven and this will be the sign
that the justice of God has as of now fixed the hour
of His great manifestation.[2] *insomuch as he causes*
fire to come down from heaven in the sight
of men.

Seventh-day Adventists are not the only ones predicting a season of calamity in the near future. So are Catholics, especially followers of the apparitions of the Virgin
Mary. Recently I read a book called *The Thunder of Justice* by Ted and Maureen Flynn. The Flynns are devout
Catholics who believe with all their hearts in their Catholic faith and in the messages given through these Marian
apparitions. They are as dedicated to their view of the
end time as any Seventh-day Adventist could possibly be.
They have made an extensive study of all the major Marian
communications of the past several hundred years and
probably many, if not most, of the minor ones as well.
Their book is a summary of what they have learned.

Most of the information in the remainder of this chapter comes from the Flynn's book. And, as I did with the
book by Michael Barkun earlier, I will abbreviate the references in this chapter to the Flynn's book as "TJ," which
stands for *The Thunder of Justice*. Endnote 1 gives the
full documentation on the book.

From their study of the Marian communications, the
Flynns see four major events in the future: A warning, a
miracle, a sign, and a chastisement. I will share with you
what each of these entails. Keep in mind that this is what
these Catholics believe, not necessarily what I believe. I will
comment on these four events after I have shared with you
what the Marian apparitions have said about them.

The warning

As Saul neared Damascus two thousand years ago, God
struck him down with a vision of Jesus and an appeal to his

conscience. This event was the turning point in Saul's life, transforming him from Saul the persecutor to Paul the apostle.

According to the apparitions of the Virgin Mary to several visionaries, a similar warning will be given to every man, woman, and child on planet Earth sometime in the near future. This warning will make each human being aware of God's existence (atheists will no longer be able to deny that there is a God), and it will reveal to each soul his or her own sins. People who are familiar with the Marian communications say that the messages of Garabandal in Spain and Medjugorje in Bosnia especially stress this future warning.

A review of what various visionaries and commentators have said about the warning gives some idea of what they believe about it:

> Every person will see himself in the burning fire of divine truth. It will be like a judgment in miniature. And then Jesus Christ will bring His glorious reign in the world (TJ, 310).

> [It will be] visible all over the world, in whatever place anyone might be. . . .
> [It will be] like the revelation of our sins, and it will be seen and felt equally by believers and non-believers and people of any religion whatsoever (TJ, 173).

> All we ever did will be before our eyes, seen all at once, in a single glance. We will know then how God's gaze crosses all barriers and grasps the utmost secrets. . . . We will understand our eternal state and the lightness or blackness of our soul.

We will suffer for a moment the pain of our sin, the pain of separation from God, the pain of purgatory or hell. We will see it all whether we wish to or not (TJ, 315).

All nations and all persons will experience it in the same way. No one will escape it (TJ, 173).

This is what Mary said to one visionary about the warning:

It will happen at 2 o'clock in the afternoon. You know the date. The sky will become very, very dark. The earth will shake. The whole world will be in turmoil. . . . People will think the world is coming to an end. The fear will be in proportion to their guilt. . . . The outpouring of my Holy Spirit will begin at the very moment they see Me (TJ, 319).

[handwritten margin note: Scary — Mary pours out the Holy Spirit — she will be seen!]

Another visionary claimed that the warning would be "a thousand times worse than earthquakes; it would be like fire but would not burn the flesh. A terrifying event would occur in the sky" (TJ, 339).

The miracle

According to the visionaries at Garabandal, a miracle will occur there "on a Thursday evening, at 8:30 p.m., between the eighth and sixteenth of March, April, or May" (TJ 162, 316). According to one of the visionaries, it will take place within one year of the warning. A visionary by the name of Conchita claims to know the exact date when the miracle will happen, but the Virgin has forbidden her to make it known to the world until eight days before its occurrence. Father Luis, whom I mentioned in the previous chapter, claimed to have been given a vision of the miracle before he died.

Visionaries have not been told the details of the miracle. However, it supposedly will be visible to millions of people at one time. And "it will support the truth that through the Body of Christ which is the Church, all graces come" (TJ, 325). "The miracle will also be Marian. It will assert the glory of the Mother of God, so that all Christians will give up their objections to her role in the Body of Christ and pay her the honor that God Himself gives her" (TJ, 325). The purpose of the miracle will be the conversion of the world. Once it occurs, human beings must convert or the most terrible catastrophe in history will come upon the world. Also, when the miracle takes place, the time of grace will end (see TJ, 326, 323).

> Unless the people heed the message of the miracle, the punishment will surely come. There will be no escape from it. The miracle will have set the fuse (TJ, 326).

The sign

Following the miracle, the visionaries say, a permanent sign will remain at Garabandal. While the visionaries have not said much about the nature of the sign, they do claim that it will be visible to anyone who wishes to come to the site to see it. No one will be able to touch it, but photographers and television crews will be able to take pictures of it. And it will defy scientific explanation. The visionaries say that the sign "will remain forever at the pines [of Garabandal]" (TJ, 162). The sign will be a call for the world to turn to holiness.

A Marian Movement of Priests has grown up around the world in recent years, and in a message dated November 12, 1981, the priests were told "that heaven is protecting with a seal all of those with God. Nothing will harm those impressed by this image" (TJ, 330). One of the messages about the seal stated:

> You are thus signed with the seal of my love, which distinguishes you from those who have allowed themselves to be seduced by the Beast and bear his imprinted blasphemous number. The Dragon and the Beast can do nothing against those who have been signed with my seal (TJ, 330).

According to one of the visionaries at Medjugorje, not everyone will be converted as a result of the warning and the miracle. "There will still be some unbelievers even when the permanent sign comes" (TJ, 332).

The chastisement

Natural disasters have occurred with increasing frequency in the world during the last few years. However, these are only a prelude to a "great chastisement" that the Marian visionaries claim is coming upon the world. People who follow the Marian apparitions closely claim that the great chastisement will be "a catastrophe described by Jesus in Matthew 24, Mark 13, and Luke 21," as well as in 2 Peter 2, 3, and in John's Apocalypse. "In these scriptural passages we have the events of the great chastisement presented in detail" (TJ, 335, 337).

It is this chastisement that Sister Agnes Sasagawa of Akita, Japan, spoke about in the opening quotation of this chapter, which I have repeated here:

> If men do not repent and better themselves, the Father will inflict a terrible punishment on all of

humanity. It will be a punishment greater than the Deluge [the Flood of Noah], such as one will never have seen before. Fire will fall from the sky and will wipe out a great part of humanity, the good as well as the bad, sparing neither priests nor faithful. The survivors will find themselves so desolate that they will envy the dead (TJ, 148, 339).

Other visionaries have said:

Clouds with lightning rays of fire and a tempest of fire will pass over the whole world and the punishment will be the most terrible ever known in the history of mankind (TJ, 351).

An unforseen fire will descend over the whole earth, and a great part of humanity will be destroyed (TJ, 351).

According to various visionaries, other phenomena associated with the chastisement will include the following:

- "The earth will go out of its orbit for three days. At that time the Second Coming of Jesus will be near. The devil will take over the world" (TJ, 341).
- "Fire will descend from Heaven and this will be a sign that the Justice of God has now fixed the hour of His great manifestation" (TJ, 341).
- "The United States will know the hour of weakness and poverty as well as 'the hour of suffering and defeat' " (TJ, 341).
- "There will be a great famine all over the world. Nothing will grow. The whole world will be hungry. All

114

will be lacking in food. The atmosphere will be changing and cause great disaster upon the earth" (TJ, 343).

- A terrible three days of darkness—exactly seventy-two hours—will come upon the earth. All the demons of hell will be let loose on the earth. Some Christians will be martyred, but the angels will take them body and soul into heaven (TJ, 347, 348).

The visionaries also claim that as a result of the chastisement, two-thirds of the human race will perish. Also, "The death of the impenitent persecutors of the Church will take place during the three days of darkness . . . so that only one fourth of mankind will survive" (TJ, 351). However, after the darkness:

> Saint Peter and Saint Paul, having come down from heaven, shall preach in the whole world and designate a new Pope. A great light will flash from their bodies and will settle upon the cardinal who is to become Pope. Christianity, then, will spread throughout the world (TJ, 353).

> In those days there will be one Shepherd and one Faith, that of the Roman Catholic Church (TJ, 354).

After the chastisement

Following the chastisement, another hour of grace will be given, providing "even the worst of the worst that have undergone the chastisements . . . the last opportunity for conversion" (TJ, 365). Then the New Jerusalem will descend to the earth, and an era of peace will follow. However, sin will not have been completely eradicated. "As children are born who have never known the previous age and its degradation, nor the warning, the miracle, or the punishment, they like all others before them will be tempted to sin" (TJ, 367). However, they will be instructed by the permanent sign at Garabandal. "It will enlighten their minds and fire their hearts to know their own sinfulness, and call them to repentance too, purifying them as they come near its glory" (TJ, 367).

Malachi Martin

I would like to conclude this Catholic description of the end time by sharing with you Malachi Martin's understanding of the vision of Fatima. Reading his book *The Keys of This Blood*, it is obvious that Martin is a firm believer in the validity of the vision of Fatima, as is John Paul II. In addition, John Paul claims to have received personal communications from heaven that confirmed the Fatima vision. Here is Martin's description of the future, seen through the "eyes" of Fatima:

> [John Paul] is waiting . . . for an event that will fission human history, splitting the immediate past from the oncoming future. It will be an event on public view in the skies, in the oceans, and on the continental landmasses of this planet. It will particularly involve our human sun. . . .
>
> Fissioning it will be as an event, in John Paul's conviction of faith, for it will immediately nullify all the grand designs the nations are now forming and will introduce the Grand Design of man's Maker. John Paul's waiting and watching time will then be over. His ministry as the Servant of the Grand Design will then begin.[3]

When will these things happen?

The visionaries say that Mary has warned them not to set dates, for "if we knew the date, people would live only waiting for the date and not convert for the love of God" (TJ, 348). Some visionaries do claim to know the dates of the warning and the miracle, but they are not allowed to reveal those dates at this time. However, from what I have read, it is very clear that many Marian followers expect these events to occur during the decade of the 1990s.

For one thing, Lucia, one of the children who received the vision of Fatima, claimed that she was told she would live to see the fulfillment of all those messages (TJ, 138). She will be 93 years old by the end of 1999. Also, the visionaries at Medjugorje claim that the virgin told them she would give them ten secrets, after which her apparitions around the world would cease and the events of the end time would begin. By 1993 two of the visionaries had received all ten secrets, and the other four had received nine of them.

Father Gobbi of Japan claims the virgin told him that "during the last decade of your century, the events which I have foretold to you will have reached their comple- tion" (TJ, 56). *now we are 2008 almost*
And one of the visionaries at Garabandal claimed that *2009* the virgin said to her:

> After Pope John XXIII died, Our Lady told me, "after Pope John, there will be three more Popes, one will reign only a short time, and then it will be the end of times." When Pope Paul VI became Pope, Our Lady mentioned this to me again. She said, "Now there will be two more Popes and then it will be the end of times, but not the end of the world" (TJ, 171).

THE COMING GREAT CALAMITY

John XXIII died in 1963. He was succeeded by Paul VI, who died in 1978. John Paul I lived only thirty-four days after becoming pope. He was succeeded by John Paul II—the third pope since John XXIII—who as of this writing is seventy-five years old and going fairly strong. John Paul has already begun making ambitious plans for celebrating a "jubilee" in the year 2,000 in Palestine. He wants this celebration to involve Christians (Catholic, Protestant, and Orthodox), Muslims, and Jews. Marian experts claim that John Paul II is to be "the Pope the Virgin spoke of at Fatima and will be the Pope who will bring into the world the Triumph of the Immaculate Heart."[4]

Analyzing the evidence

This is an overview of end-time events as proposed by the visionaries who claim to have communicated with the Virgin Mary. What should we as Seventh-day Adventists make of it all?

First, I believe we need to recognize that we also have been given an overview of the end time, first in Scripture, and in even greater detail in the writings of Ellen White. We must trust these sources above any supposed apparitions of a Virgin Mary who has long since died and been buried.

Second, I believe there is a certain sensationalism to the claims of these Marian visionaries. Thus we need to avoid taking them too seriously, especially the details. This is particularly true in light of the inspired evidence that we already have. We must avoid drawing conclusions about the future from sources that as far as we are concerned come from the enemy of God. We should especially avoid making too much of their predictions that the events of the end time will come before the year 2,000. It is certainly possible, of course, that the final crisis will begin before the end of the millennium. My point is that we must avoid working ourselves into a fever of end-time excitement on the strength of what a supposed Virgin Mary has said to her followers.

However—and this is my third point—Satan is even more aware than we are of what lies ahead, and I believe that through these so-called apparitions of the Virgin Mary he is preparing his forces for the final conflict. These Marian predictions are set up as a foil, so that when the real events occur, people will increase faith in Mary.

While it is true that an element of sensationalism exists among Catholics in all the talk about Fatima and apparitions of the Virgin Mary, it is also true that hundreds of thousands and probably millions of people believe that the things I have shared with you in this chapter and the previous one are true. Satan doesn't care how sensational people get, so long as they believe what he wants them to believe.

I also find a significant similarity between our own view of the end time and the Catholic view that I have shared with you in this chapter. Adventists, as you know, are quite famous for charts about the end time. I've created a few of them myself over the years. Here is a chart of the end time that is based on the Catholic view that we have been discussing:

	The miracle	The sign	End of grace		Second coming
The warning			The tribulation The chastisement		

Now compare this with a similar chart that shows the events of the end time as understood by Seventh-day Adventists:

THE COMING GREAT CALAMITY

	Close of probation		Second coming
The loud cry The final warning		The time of trouble The seven last plagues	

Notice that in each of these charts there is a final warning, an end to God's grace (what Adventists call "the close of probation"[5]), and a time of great trouble between the end of God's grace and Christ's second coming. This similarity is not a mere coincidence. I believe it is part of another master plan for the end time that is patterned after God's great plan.

There are several other similarities between the Adventist understanding about the end time and these Catholic ideas. Perhaps you noticed a few pages back a hint about an end-time seal for God's people that resembles our own teaching on this point. Also, the three days of darkness near the conclusion of the chastisement is very similar to Ellen White's description of a great darkness that falls on the world just before the second coming of Christ (see *The Great Controversy*, 635, 636).

And in this book I have suggested that the falling of the stars predicted by Jesus may refer to comets, asteroids, and/or meteorites. Ellen White also spoke of balls of fire falling on the earth. These ideas bear a striking similarity to those of Sister Agnes Sasagawa of Akita, whom I quoted at the beginning of this chapter: "Fire will fall from the sky and will wipe out a great part of humanity." There is also some resemblance between what I have said in this book and Malachi Martin's statement about "an event on public view in the skies, in the oceans, and on the continental landmasses of this planet" that will "particularly involve our human sun."

I also believe that we can expect something to happen in the future to fulfill the Marian expectation of a miracle and a great sign. Ellen White herself predicted that "fearful sights of a supernatural character will soon be revealed in the heavens, in token of the power of miracle-working demons" (*The Great Controversy*, 624). Surely some of these will be interpreted by Marian followers as a fulfillment of their prediction of a coming miracle followed by a great sign.

I will conclude this chapter by examining a quotation from the Marian publication *Queen of Peace* and one further Marian "revelation." Again, please notice the similarity of some of these ideas and our own Adventist understanding:

> The Virgin says this Era of Mercy [the time in which we now live] is headed into a decisive stage. Repeatedly, Mary has told visionaries that God is going to give the world signs to return to Him, great miracles and perhaps the sight of Christ Himself. . . . Other miracles will be of such grand design that it is said only obstinate sinners will be able to deny them.
>
> Marian followers say these miracles will be worldwide and given so 'that all may believe.' . . . After the miracles, visionaries say, the world will be cleansed of all who choose to remain attached to evil and sin.[6] *(the heretics who aren't Catholic)*

This statement contains hints of Satan's final great deception, when he personates Christ. It also contains a guarded suggestion of a future death decree against dissenters. And in that same vein, notice the following statement dating back to the Marian apparitions at La Salette, France, in 1846:

THE COMING GREAT CALAMITY

Then Jesus Christ, in an act of His justice and His great mercy will command His angels to have all His enemies put to death. Suddenly, the persecutors of the Church of Jesus Christ and all those given over to sin will perish and the earth will become desert-like. And then peace will be made, and man will be reconciled with God. Jesus Christ will be served, worshiped, and glorified. Charity will flourish everywhere (TJ, 114).

Need I say more?

---

1. Ted and Maureen Flynn, *The Thunder of Justice* (Sterling, Virginia: Maxkol Communications, 1993), 148.
2. Ibid., 148, 149.
3. Malachi Martin, *The Keys of This Blood* (New York: Simon and Schuster, 1990), 639.
4. *Queen of Peace: Special Edition III* (McKees Rocks, Pennsylvania: Pittsburgh Center for Peace, 1995), 2.
5. In some languages of the world, including Spanish, the English expression "close of probation" is actually translated "end of the time of grace."
6. *Queen of Peace*, 13.

CHAPTER TWELVE

DISASTERS AND THE CRISIS
in Revelation 13

For many years I had a hard time understanding how Revelation 13 could possibly be fulfilled in the world of the late twentieth century. I did not doubt the prophecy. I just could not fit it in with the world in which I lived. I now know that I don't have to fit it in with the world in which I live, because Revelation 13 won't be fulfilled in the world in which I live. I am writing these words in December 1995, but Revelation 13 will be fulfilled in a world that is vastly different from the world of 1995. I have already discussed with you the worldwide paradigm shift that must happen before Revelation 13 can be fulfilled. Now I would like to share with you some additional thoughts about the world of the future.

Several years ago, I read a book called *The Addictive Organization*. I did not purchase the book with the intention of improving my understanding of Bible prophecy, and when I began reading it, I had no idea that it would contribute significantly to my understanding Revelation 13 and 17. But so it happened.

The authors pointed out that one evidence of a dysfunctional (addictive) organization is the way in which its managers handle crises. Please read their description:

> In [times of] crisis we allow people to take over and enact unusual procedures. Crisis feeds on the illusion that control can bring the situation under control. Crises are used to excuse drastic and erratic actions on the part of managers. . . . Individuals have fewer responsibilities in crisis as management gathers power to ride out the problem. When crisis is the norm, management tends to assume an unhealthy amount of power on a daily basis.

Above all else, Revelation 13 is about a crisis and how the world will relate to that crisis. However, here's an extremely significant point: Revelation 13 does not say that there is a crisis, and it gives us almost no information about the nature of the crisis. That is "behind the scenes." *All Revelation 13 shows us is the world's response to the crisis*, and by examining the response carefully, we can recognize the existence of a crisis. Perhaps a little made-up story will help you to understand what I mean.

A man worked as a supervisor in a factory, and he had twenty-five employees under him. He thoroughly enjoyed his job, because management gave him a great deal of discretion to move his employees around in order to use their efforts in the most efficient way for the good of the company.

One day when he came to work, the supervisor found a sealed envelope on his desk marked "personal." Inside was a letter from the president stating that beginning immediately, management would be taking greater responsibility for assigning his employees their daily tasks. His job would be to carry out management's wishes. Naturally, the supervisor wondered what he had done that caused management to question his performance.

Before he had time to get too worried, though, a supervisor from a neighboring department came into his office and handed him a letter just like the one he had received. A quick check around the plant showed that all lower-level managers and many middle- and upper-level managers had received the same instructions. Everyone wondered what was going on, but the letters didn't hint at the reason.

A couple of days later everyone's responsibility was curtailed even further. Over the next two weeks all the supervisors had more and more of their authority stripped away, until they were little more than company robots, doing what they were told. Yet nobody down in the factory had a clue as to what was happening upstairs.

This story is obviously fictitious, because in any normal company, the grapevine would be alive with rumors about what was happening upstairs and why. However, for the purpose of our illustration, it's important that nobody has any idea what's going on.

We needn't be totally in the dark about the problem in our fictitious factory though. Having read the quotation from *The Addictive Organization* that I shared with you, we can be certain of one thing: There was a crisis in the boardroom.

THE COMING GREAT CALAMITY

How can we be so sure?

Because "when crisis is the norm, management tends to assume an unhealthy amount of power on a daily basis," and "individuals have fewer responsibilities in crisis as management gathers power to ride out the problem." Even if no one has told us there is a crisis, we can surmise it from the evidence out in the factory: the way management is taking responsibility away from lower-level supervisors and gathering power to itself. This points unmistakably to a crisis in the president's office, even if we don't know what it is.

The crisis in Revelation 13

A careful look at Revelation 13 shows us a similar situation: The world's "managers"—two beasts—are gathering power to themselves:

- *The first beast "was given authority over every tribe, people, language and nation"* (verse 7). This beast controls the whole world!
- *The first beast "was given power to make war against the saints"* (verse 7). In its effort to consolidate power, the beast is trying to get rid of all opposition.
- *The second beast "caused all who refused to worship the image [to the beast] to be killed"* (verse 15). This beast uses the threat of death to consolidate power. It is putting forth the most extreme effort to get rid of all opposition.
- *The second beast also forced everyone . . . to receive a mark or suffer economic boycott* (verses 16, 17). The beast uses the power of the economy as a means to stifle all opposition.

The basic issue in Revelation 13 is global control. The two beast powers are trying desperately to get rid of all opposition and consolidate power to themselves. Why? Even though Revelation 13 does not say so, the extreme effort of the two beasts to gain global control is a clear indication that planet Earth is in a terrible crisis, and these beast powers capitalize on the situation by seizing power and enforcing their policies as a means to bring things back under control.

Of course, the two beasts have more than the world's welfare in mind in their grasp for power. They also have a very immoral personal agenda to advance. The evidence for this lies in the fact that the second beast will deceive earth's inhabitants with "great and miraculous signs" (verses 13, 14). In other words, the methods this beast uses to gain power are highly unethical. Another name for this is manipulation. Manipulation generally works only when the persons being manipulated are unaware of what's happening to them. Thus deception is a key element in manipulative techniques for controlling others. And that, I suggest, is what's going on in the second beast's deceptive miraculous signs.

Another significant evidence that a crisis exists behind the scenes in Revelation 13 is the response of the vast majority of the world's people. To understand this detail in Revelation 13, we need to go back to our fictitious story about the crisis in the factory.

The only thing the people in that story knew was that management had taken away their power. From this they could deduce that a crisis had developed in the front office, but they had no idea what it was. I used this illustration to help you understand my point that Revelation 13 does not inform *you and me*, who are reading the story ahead of time, about the crisis that enables these beasts

[handwritten margin note: truth is not allowed to shine out & expose the deception]

to seize power. However, every person who is alive upon the earth at the time these events actually happen will be painfully aware of the crisis. And in their panic they will submit to two highly authoritarian powers that under today's more normal circumstances they would resist mightily.

This, I propose, is the backdrop to verses 3 and 4, which tell us that earth's inhabitants were "astonished and followed the beast," and they "worshiped the beast." Furthermore, not only is the beast grasping for power, but the people seem quite willing to let the beast have it, for verse 7 says that the beast "was *given* power."

The fact that the people are so willing to follow the beast and to give it power and authority is yet another evidence of a terrible worldwide crisis.

Even though Revelation 13 says next to nothing about the crisis that is going on behind the scenes, the Bible does not leave us totally in the dark about it. Jesus gave us some important details in His sermon on the signs of the end of the world. From Luke's account of Jesus' sermon, we learn that the nations will be in anguish and perplexity over the signs in the heavens, and the whole human race will be in a state of terror (see Luke 21:25, 26). And Matthew tells us about a coming time of distress so severe that it would wipe out the human race if God didn't cut it short (see Matthew 24:21, 22).

That sounds like a crisis to me! No wonder Ellen White spoke of a "last great crisis" and "the crisis of the ages" that is coming on the world (*Testimonies for the Church*, 9:11; *Prophets and Kings*, 278). This crisis will create the powerful paradigm shift I spoke about in chapter 1, which will turn over political control of the entire world to the two beast powers.

Putting it all together

I'd like now to bring together several of the ideas we've discussed in this book. You will recall from our discussion in a couple of earlier chapters that millenarian movements arise out of crises and natural disasters. Disaster opens people's minds to new explanations of reality, which is the intellectual stuff of which millenarian movements are made.

You will also recall, however, that millenarian movements do not create the new explanation of reality out of thin air at the time the disaster occurs. The new explanation must be present in the environment before the disaster occurs. Most people will have rejected it—perhaps even scoffed at the kooks who were advocating it. That doesn't matter. In fact, the scoffing may be an aid in starting the new millenarian movement. Because in spite of their scoffing, *the new explanation will be in the people's minds*, and when the disaster occurs, suddenly something will "click," and they will say, "Ah-ha! So the kooks were right after all!"

A global paradigm shift occurs when people all over the world respond like that to a crisis. That's also how a millenarian movement is born.

Now please think of this: The terrible crisis in the world just before Jesus returns will create, not one, but two powerful millenarian movements. Each of these movements will have its own explanation for what is happening. Indeed, each will already have proclaimed its explanation to the world long before the crisis arises. Thus each movement's ideological raw material will already be in place at the time the crisis arises, providing the intellectual foundation on which its millenarian movement can spring up and grow.

One of these millenarian movements will be "the remnant" of Revelation 12:17 who "keep the commandments of God, and have the testimony of Jesus" (KJV). This is the millenarian movement that you and I are familiar with as Seventh-day Adventists. And we have been spreading our ideological raw material all over the world for more than one hundred and fifty years.

Perhaps you never thought of the beast powers of Revelation 13 as a millenarian movement, but I propose that that is exactly what they will be. And the intellectual raw material around which that millenarian movement is organized will be the information that I shared with you in the previous two chapters about apparitions of the Virgin Mary and "her" predictions of terrible natural disasters in the near future.

Let's look again at the characteristics of a millenarian movement that we read about earlier in this book and compare them with the two millenarian movements that will arise during earth's final crisis.

- *Millenarians believe that salvation is imminent.* This is true of both Seventh-day Adventists and of those Catholics who are strong advocates of Marian apparitions.
- *Millenarians expect that in the near future the present social order will be completely destroyed and a perfect society will be established.* Seventh-day Adventists certainly believe that, and in the previous chapter you read that Marian Catholics believe exactly the same thing.
- *Millenarians believe that their efforts will hasten the destruction of the old order and the establishment of the new.* This also is true of both Adventists and Marian Catholics.
- *Millenarians claim to have total truth.* Again, this is

true of both Adventists and Marian Catholics.

- *Millenarians have a belief system that explains life's ultimate questions*. The Adventist and Catholic belief systems are poles apart, but that's not the point. We each have a belief system that explains life's ultimate questions.
- *Millenarians demand total commitment to their cause*. Catholics are at least as insistent on this point as Adventists, and some of them are probably far more insistent than many of us.
- *Millenarians claim to be a "remnant"—a small group of righteous people in a world that is totally evil*. This is perhaps the one point on which Adventists and Catholics differ, for the simple reason that Catholics can hardly claim to be a *small* group. However, they do claim to be a group of righteous people in a world that is totally evil.

Also, please notice that each of these movements is predicting terrible natural disasters. In fact, at the present time Marian Catholics are carrying this particular message to the world far more actively than Adventists are. Ask yourself, for example, when was the last time you heard an Adventist sermon or read a book (other than this one) or magazine article about the judgments of God that are coming on the world.

The great controversy in Revelation

One of the primary reasons why God gave us the book of Revelation was to help us understand the great controversy between Christ and Satan and especially to help us understand the final phase of that conflict, just before Jesus returns to this earth.

Revelation 12:17 introduces us to one of two parties

that will lock in mortal combat: God's remnant. Revelation 13 then describes the conflict between God's remnant and the apostate beast powers of the earth.

I just explained to you that during earth's final days God's remnant and the apostate beast powers will both become powerful millenarian movements. This means that the two millenarian movements of the end time will be locked in a life-and-death struggle that can only end in the total destruction of one of them. The beast powers will put forth superhuman efforts to destroy God's people, and for a time it will appear that they are winning, for Revelation says that the first beast of chapter 13 will be given power "to make war against the saints *and to conquer them*" (Revelation 13:7).

The language of Revelation 13 is highly symbolical, and its terms are very spiritual. Thus it is easy for you and me to discuss the world that it predicts in abstract terms. The truth is, however, that the events of the future will strike us with terrible reality—"with blinding force," as Ellen White put it on one occasion (*Selected Messages*, 2:142).

We're talking here about arrests and court appearances, loss of employment, imprisonment, and in some cases the firing squad, for the sake of the truth. Ultimately, we are talking about a crisis so severe that every one of God's people will be found either in a prison cell or hidden away in some damp cellar or dark cave. They won't be able to so much as show their faces in public places to buy food and clothes, because they will be destined to execution. Every one of them, all over the world.

However, at the very darkest moment, when it appears that they have no way of escape, God will intervene to deliver His people. For Revelation 19:20 tells us that the beast will be "thrown alive into the fiery lake of burning sulphur."

MARVIN MOORE

I don't know when the season of calamity that precipitates the final crisis will begin. However, I don't have to. Far more important for you and me today is to prepare for that crisis. For when it comes, I want to be on the winning side, and I know you do too. The question is, how can we ensure that we are on that side?

---

* Anne Wilson Schaef and Diane Fassel, *The Addictive Organization* (San Francisco: Harper Collins, 1988), 160.

CHAPTER THIRTEEN

OUR RESPONSIBILITY
to the world

Do you feel afraid to share your faith with your neighbors and friends, yet guilty because you don't? Do you hear two little voices inside you—one saying you should and the other telling you people would be offended if you did?

Join the crowd.

Actually, I believe we need to listen to both of these voices. The voice that tells us that people would be offended if we approached them about our faith may be trying to give us an important message. One hundred years ago it was quite acceptable to discuss and even debate one's religious views with others. But today, religion has come to be considered almost as private a matter as sex. Just as we don't run around talking about our sexual practices with everyone we meet, so we are not supposed to talk about our religious faith with everyone we meet. Some people have even complained about "religious harassment" on the job, which led the Equal Employment Opportunities Commission a while back to briefly consider adding "religious harassment" to its list of taboos in the workplace.

I sense this problem in my own attitude toward sharing my faith with others. And to a certain extent, this is OK. I believe that in every endeavor to tell others what we believe, we must be sensitive to the cultural climate in which we live.

However, this does not mean that we must ignore the other voice inside us, urging us to share our faith. Rather, we must look for ways to fulfill Jesus' Great Commission that will be as acceptable as possible within our culture.

When dealing with relatives and neighbors, I believe it's important that we find tactful ways for opening up opportunities to share our faith and then give them the choice of responding or not. For example, my wife and I decided some time back to send *Signs of the Times* to our neighbors, and my wife wanted to send the magazine to the people in the government office where she works. However, rather than just sending in their names and addresses, we obtained several copies of a recent issue and took them around to our neighbors with a little note tucked in each magazine that said, "If you would like to receive a free subscription, write or call us." My wife also passed the magazines around at work.

Among the eight or so homes on our street where we left the magazine, one responded favorably, and two or three of my wife's colleagues at work said they would appreciate receiving a subscription.

My mother-in-law had a tactful way to share her faith with her neighbors. She went to every home on her street, but she did not knock on the door. She just left the first lesson of the Voice of Prophecy Bible study guides rolled between the knob and the door jamb. Inside each one

THE COMING GREAT CALAMITY

was a little note saying that she would be back on such and such a day, and if they liked lesson 1, she would be glad to leave lesson 2. Only on the second visit did she knock on doors, and all she asked was, "Did you receive lesson 1? Would you like to receive lesson 2?" This was a tactful approach that gave the people freedom of choice.

One woman responded positively, and my mother-in-law rejoiced a few months later when she was baptized.

Plain old-fashioned friendship is one of the most important ways to witness for Jesus. After my wife and I moved to Idaho in 1985, we often walked our two dogs on the street during the evening when many of our neighbors were in their front yards or out on the street. It was easy to stop and chat with them, and we thoroughly enjoyed living in that neighborhood. We had no idea what kind of an impression we were making till one day an Adventist friend shared an experience he had had with a woman who worked in his office. This woman lived three doors down the street from us, and we had had a number of friendly chats with her and her husband. She told our Adventist friend that "if I ever join a church, it will be the Adventist Church."

We felt good about that.

Should we talk to our friends about the actual judgments of God that are coming upon the world? I believe it is appropriate that we do so when we can do it tactfully. I am reminded of Ellen White's statement about balls of fire that I quoted in an earlier chapter. The people were terrified at these judgments from God, but God's people were saying, "Praise the Lord."

"Why are you praising the Lord?" inquired those upon whom was coming sudden destruction?"

"Because we now see what we have been looking for."

"If you believed these things were coming, why did you not tell us?" was the terrible response. "We did not know about these things. Why did you leave us in ignorance? Again and again you have seen us; why did you not become acquainted with us, and tell us of the judgment to come, and that we must serve God, lest we perish? Now we are lost!" (*Reflecting Christ*, 143).

In an earlier chapter I pointed out Barkun's conclusion that "foreknowledge [of a disaster] is likely not only to mitigate the disaster effects but also make a millenarian reaction less probable"; and "the more one prepares for future contingencies, the less likely that these contingencies will inflict disorganizing damage." If this is true—and I am sure it is—then isn't it important that we let non-Adventists as well as Adventists know that these calamities are coming?

"But I'd feel foolish talking to my friends about these things," you may protest. "They wouldn't believe me."

I will respond to this apprehension in two ways. First, let's assume that your concern is valid. It really doesn't matter that people may reject what you and I tell them right now. What matters is that they have the information about the coming disasters in their heads so that when the disasters come they will know how to interpret them. Remember Barkun's statement that "disaster produces the questioning, the anxiety, and the suggestibility that are required [for change]; only in its wake are people moved to abandon old values of the past" (*Disaster and the Millennium*, 6). It doesn't really matter whether your friends think you are "kooky" today, because when these events happen they'll say, "Maybe the kooks were right after all!"

However, in today's world we do not have to fear being

thought of as kooks for telling people that terrible calamities will be coming on the world *in the future*. These calamities are happening *right now!* Two of the most destructive hurricanes in recent history struck Florida and Hawaii in 1993. Unprecedented floods occurred in the Midwestern United States in 1994. At about the same time, terrible firestorms occurred in Los Angeles and Sydney, Australia. And powerful earthquakes struck in Northridge, California, in 1994, and Kobe, Japan, in 1995. Who knows how many natural disasters will have occurred around the world by the time you read these words.

I can assure you that the Marian literature I have read emphasizes these very disasters as signs that God is trying to warn people to mend their ways. Ellen White informed us one hundred years ago that these calamities were coming. We have had a commission from God for one hundred and fifty years to warn the world about the coming crisis. Why should we be more afraid or less active than our Catholic friends in accomplishing this task—or is God going to have to let them do it for us?

We don't even have to be ashamed to talk to people about balls of fire. Since about 1990, scientists have increasingly been warning the world of the danger our planet faces from comets, asteroids, and meteorites. It's not a question of *whether* some of these objects will strike us, they say, but only of *when*.

In today's climate, when religion is a taboo subject for discussion, Ellen White's balls of fire are actually an excellent way to bring up a discussion about spiritual and religious issues with our nonreligious friends. I don't mean that we should quote Ellen White to them. All we have to do is wait for the subject of asteroids to come up on the evening news or perhaps in our newspaper or news magazine, then ask our friends what they think about it all. After they share their opinion with us, we can tell them what we believe is coming. And we needn't hesitate to tell them that our belief is based on Bible prophecy. In spite of the very secular world in which we live, a large percentage of people in America and Canada continue to be very interested in prophecy.

I would also encourage our pastors and evangelists to discuss these things in their public meetings. I believe comets, asteroids, and meteorites would make an excellent advertising topic to draw a crowd. Everyone is aware of them these days. Tell people that in your meetings you will share with them what the Bible says about these invaders from outer space. I can assure you that, having already heard about these things from the scientists, many people will *want* to know what God says about them.

I would urge, however, that we present these ideas as possibilities and not as absolute facts about the future of our planet. For one thing, we can't say for sure that these things *will happen*. And in any case, it's not so important that people actually believe these things are coming. What matters is that they have an awareness of the possibility. Then, even if they laugh at the idea right now, should the comets and asteroids actually come, the people will know what these events mean and how to relate to them.

I believe we must be serious in sharing with others the information we have about the end time. Satan is doing everything he can to cause people to lose eternal life, and his effort will be especially intense during earth's final conflict. One of the most important reasons why we exist as a church is to prepare the world for the second coming of Christ and the events leading up to it so that they, along with us, can pass through that time without being deceived.

I urge each Seventh-day Adventist to pray for opportunities to share what you know about the end time with those who are not aware of it.

CHAPTER FOURTEEN

PREPARING
for the
Disasters Ahead

Earlier in this book I shared with you what I believe is the most significant statement Ellen White ever made about the coming judgments of God. It is found in her book *Christ's Object Lessons*, in the chapter about the ten virgins. Here is her statement:

> It is in a crisis that character is revealed. When the earnest voice proclaimed at midnight, "Behold, the bridegroom cometh; go ye out to meet him," and the sleeping virgins were roused from their slumbers, it was seen who had made preparation for the event. Both parties were taken unawares; but one was prepared for the emergency, and the other was found without preparation. So now, *a sudden and unlooked-for calamity*, something that brings the soul face to face with death, will show whether there is any real faith in the promises of God. It will show whether the soul is

sustained by grace. The great final test comes at the close of human probation, when it will be too late for the soul's need to be supplied (412, emphasis supplied).

More than any other statement Ellen White made about the coming judgments of God, this paragraph tells us how to prepare for that crisis. Please follow through with me as we analyze what she says.

The shaking

One of Ellen White's more common themes, when she talked about the end time, was what she called a "shaking" that is coming among God's people. This expression probably comes out of Ezekiel 38:19 in the King James Version: "For in my jealousy and in the fire of my wrath have I spoken, Surely in that day there shall be a great shaking in the land of Israel" (emphasis supplied).

Ellen White understood the shaking to be a time when the events of the future will create such a terrible crisis for God's people that many will abandon their faith and join the ranks of the enemy. Here are a couple of representative statements:

> The days are fast approaching when there will be great perplexity and confusion. Satan, clothed in angel robes, will deceive, if possible, the very elect. There will be gods many and lords many. Every wind of doctrine will be blowing. . . . The Lord has faithful servants, who in the shaking, testing time will be disclosed to view (*Testimonies for the Chruch*, 5:80).

> Every trial made by the refining, purifying process upon professed Christians proves some to

be dross. The fine gold does not always appear. In every religious crisis some fall under temptation. The shaking of God blows away multitudes like dry leaves. Prosperity multiplies a mass of professors. Adversity purges them out of the church. As a class, their spirits are not steadfast with God. They go out from us because they are not of us; for when tribulation or persecution arises because of the word, many are offended (ibid., 4:89).

The shaking is a time when trial will separate true Christians from those who merely make a profession of Christianity. In the first statement, Ellen White equates the shaking time with the "testing time." Our loyalty to God's truth and our commitment to remain loyal to Jesus will be severely tested by the traumatic events of the end time.

Several statements in Revelation 13 suggest this same idea:

- "All inhabitants of the earth will worship the beast— all whose names have not been written in the book of life belonging to the Lamb" (verse 8).
- "He was given power to give breath to the image of the first beast, so that it could speak and cause all who refused to worship the image to be killed" (verse 15).
- "No one could buy or sell unless he had the mark, which is the name of the beast or the number of his name" (verse 17).

The point of these brief statements from Revelation is that there will be two classes of people upon the earth at the end of time. One group will be loyal to God, and the other group will try to force them to give up their loyalty to God. This trial will cause many people to leave us. *This will be the shaking.*

Now let's come back to Ellen White's statement in *Christ's Object Lessons* about the ten virgins. She is talking about the shaking time, even though she doesn't use the word. Notice the division of Christians into two classes:

> When the earnest voice proclaimed at midnight, "Behold, the bridegroom cometh; go ye out to meet him," and the sleeping virgins were roused from their slumbers, it was seen who had made preparation for the event. Both parties were taken unawares; but one was prepared for the emergency, and the other was found without preparation.

In this statement, the two classes of Christians are defined as those who are spiritually prepared for the final crisis and those who are not. Those who are prepared will remain loyal to God. Those who are not will join the ranks of the apostasy.

In Christ's parable it is the midnight cry that awakens the sleeping virgins and shows who is prepared and who is not. Ellen White applies this midnight cry in our day to the final crisis, when God will allow the disasters that we have been discussing in this book to fall upon the world. She says, "So now, a sudden and unlooked-for calamity . . . will show whether there is any real faith in the promises of God."

Character the real test

Exactly what is it that will separate those who are loyal to God from those who are not? Ellen White gives us a couple of significant suggestions.

THE COMING GREAT CALAMITY

"It is in a crisis that character is revealed," she said. When the midnight cry woke the girls up, half were prepared and the other half were not, and *character was the determining factor*. In the end time, it may seem that the calamity is the real issue, because the whole world will be in such a panic about it. However, character will actually be the real issue. Yet the calamity will be important, because that is what will reveal character.

And what aspect of character will the calamity reveal? Strength of will to endure hardship, perhaps, or a determination to press on against all odds? No. Ellen White said that it will show whether there is any real faith in the promises of God. *Key*

Ellen White also says the calamity will bring God's people face to face with death. However, the calamity itself is not the danger (though some of God's people may perish in the destruction it causes). The threat of death will arise out of the world's response to the calamity. As disasters multiply around the globe, the world will experience a profound paradigm shift that once again places spiritual, religious forces in control of earth's political systems. Two powerful millenarian movements will arise that are at bitter enmity with each other,[1] and one of them will persecute God's people ferociously. *Cain + Able / Jacob + Esau*

It is this persecution that will reveal who has developed a strong character and who has not. This persecution will test the character of every human being, and the issue will be faith in the promises of God.

What is sin?

Let's deviate a moment and discuss a major controversy that is going on in the Adventist Church today. This debate has to do with the nature of sin and the kind of preparation God's people must make in order to be ready for the end time. On one side are those who say that sin is basically what we *do*—the behavioral choices we make. And they quote texts such as James 4:17 to nail down the point: "To him that knoweth to do good, and doeth it not, to him it is sin" (KJV).

On the other side are those who say that sin is essentially what we *are*. They do not deny that wrong behavior is sinful, but they affirm that the behavioral choices we humans make arise out of what we are on the inside; they are a reflection of our character. Those on this side of the debate quote passages such as Mark 2:23, where Jesus said that evil "come[s] from inside and make[s] a man 'unclean.'"

These two views of sin have everything to do with the kind of preparation we will make for the end time. Those who think of sin primarily as wrong behavior will make every effort to learn what is right and wrong to *do*; they will focus their attention on making right behavioral choices.

On the other hand, those who view sin primarily as a condition of the mind and heart will focus their attention on cultivating their inner spiritual life and developing their character. This does not mean they will consider right and wrong behavioral choices to be unimportant. But they will recognize that correcting their wrong behavior depends more on having a godly character than on the choices they make at any given moment. Those who have a right character *will make the right behavioral choices.*

I do not hesitate to say that Ellen White comes down on the side of character development as the key issue in preparing for the final crisis, for it is character that will separate the wheat from the chaff in the testing time, not just behavior. "It is in a crisis that *character* is revealed," she said, not that *behavior* is revealed. This is not to say that the testing time won't reveal behavior too. It most certainly will. The behavior of those who have not developed a strong character will be very evident: They will abandon their faith. They will join the ranks of the enemy. They could hardly make a worse behavioral choice! But their choice of behavior will arise out of what they have come to be on the inside. *Therefore, the key preparation God's people need to be making today in anticipation of the final crisis is character development*.

Unfortunately, character development is such an involved issue that I cannot go into detail about it in this book. Fortunately, I have already written a whole book on that subject, and I urge you to obtain a copy. The title is *Conquering the Dragon Within*.[2] My primary focus in that book is on how to cultivate the inner life, with a strong emphasis on behavior change as well.

As you develop your character, I recommend that you make trust in God a major focus of your effort. I say this because of Ellen White's statement that the final crisis "will show whether there is any real faith in the promises of God." If you are one of those people who has a tough time enduring tough times—if you "suffer" a lot and perhaps complain a lot about the trials you have to put up with—then I can guarantee that you will have a *really* tough time in the final crisis. For only those who have learned to trust God in and through their trials will have the character they need to endure the final crisis.

This is the most important preparation you and I can make for the season of calamity that is coming.

Getting correct information

Surviving the end time will also require having a correct understanding of what's happening in the world, because advance knowledge will help us to be prepared for

[handwritten margin notes:] Key Key

[handwritten note at bottom:] What I eat is behavioral trials come on their own — trusting God in them is the key — then my behaviors will fall into line.

the emergency. In his book *Disaster and the Millennium*,[3] which I quoted extensively in a couple of earlier chapters, Michael Barkun makes some comments that I find to be quite relevant in this regard:

> Much of the force of a disaster comes from the sudden manner in which it assaults unprepared societies, institutions, and psyches. The more one prepares for future contingencies, the less likely that these contingencies will inflict disorganizing damage. Even where uncontrollable forces of nature are concerned, the mere existence of forewarning constitutes a defense (57).

> Foreknowledge is likely not only to mitigate the disaster effects but also make a millenarian reaction less probable. Such information deprives the event of its shock value and defends the environment against excessive disruption—both of which deprive millenarian movements of their reasons for existence (ibid., 59).

In the first statement, Michael Barkun says that "the more one prepares for future contingencies, the less likely that these contingencies will inflict disorganizing damage." That's a rather technical way of stating what Ellen White said in *Christ's Object Lessons:* "Both parties were taken unawares; but one was prepared for the emergency, and the other was found without preparation." The "disorganizing damage" we need to protect against from Ellen White's perspective would be apostasy—being shaken out of the faith that can save and joining the opposition. Barkun says that knowing ahead of time that the destructive judgment is coming helps to prevent that reaction:

THE COMING GREAT CALAMITY

"Such information deprives the event of its shock value and defends the environment against excessive disruption—both of which deprive millenarian movements of their reasons for existence."

Those who do not have this advance information will be taken by surprise, and this will put them in great danger of abandoning their faith. For one of the major points of Barkun's book is that disaster opens people's minds to ideas that formerly they would have rejected.

I can assure you that this will be a danger to God's people. The vast majority of the world will accept the explanation of "the other" millenarian movement. I expect that there will be a great union of all religious faiths that is at least partially influenced by the apparitions of the supposed "mother of God" that we discussed in an earlier chapter.[4] As calamities multiply and the crisis deepens, the threat of persecution will be added to the popular movement toward religious union, and the pressure for God's people to yield their faith will be intense.

Today, prior to the crisis of the end time with its disasters, nearly all Seventh-day Adventists take a firm stand against certain teachings that are quite popular in other churches. But the disasters of the end time will be just as likely to "open" some of our minds to consider favorably those ideas we now reject as the other way around. That's exactly what Barkun is saying. That's what Ellen White is saying. That's what the shaking will be all about.

In anticipation of this danger, one of the best ways we can protect our own people from joining the opposition is to inform them about the disasters that are coming. For, as Barkun points out, foreknowledge will make it easier to adjust to the disaster, and it will also make a millenarian reaction toward the other side less probable.

The apostle Paul warned about the danger of natural disasters to religious faith:

> When people are saying, "Peace and safety," destruction will come on them suddenly, as labor pains on a pregnant woman, and they will not escape (1 Thessalonians 5:3).

Notice that it is the suddenness of the destruction that Paul said will catch people in Satan's trap. Those who are trapped had been saying, "Peace and safety," so they obviously had no idea what was coming. The suddenness of the disaster combined with their lack of foreknowledge about it creates a situation in which they are highly susceptible to a change in their belief system, and they will apostatize. That is Paul's point. But notice what he says next:

> But you, brothers, are not in darkness so that this day should surprise you like a thief (1 Thessalonians 5:4).

Paul says that God's people need not be "in the dark" about the sudden destruction that is coming on the world! That is why we need to be informing our own people about the events of future, for *those who are informed will not be taken by surprise*. They will have advance knowledge of the calamities, and they will be able to work these terrible events into their biblical and prophetic understanding. Foreknowledge will be a protection against disorientation and the danger of changing belief systems and joining the false millenarian movement.

We can say, then, that while character development is the most important preparation we can make for the coming crisis, we also can profit from awareness that these disasters are coming, for foreknowledge will help us to retain, and even strengthen, our faith.

Commitment to Bible truth

In her book *The Great Controversy*, Ellen White said that "so closely will the counterfeit resemble the true that it will be impossible to distinguish between them except by the Holy Scriptures. By their testimony every statement and every miracle must be tested" (593).

I realized the importance of these words as I was studying some of the Catholic literature about the Virgin Mary and Marian apparitions. One author, writing in a Catholic publication called *Mary's People*, said:

> Protestantism's new emphasis on securing a biblical foundation for every belief and practice led to a questioning of dogmas such as the Immaculate Conception and the Assumption among other things. . . . [Thus] there was some eroding of Mary's position in the minds of the Protestant reformers, many of whom felt that everything must be explicitly found in Scripture if it is to be believed.[5] *Shouldn't it be? yes, yes, yes Scripture*

The author then goes on to suggest that non-Catholic readers take a new look at the Catholic doctrine of Mary. He concludes by saying:

> Perhaps as Mary becomes a focal point of new discussions, leaders from all quarters of the Christian world community will recognize her importance.[6]

oh boy

The point I want you to notice is the logical, theological foundation of this author's argument. He begins by questioning the Protestant principle of finding a scriptural foundation for every belief and practice, and on that basis he encourages Protestants to take a new look at the Catholic doctrine of Mary. Perhaps the most startling aspect of this statement is that it was written by a Lutheran clergyman! Yet it was Luther who first took a stand on "the Bible and the Bible alone" as the basis for all faith and practice.

This underscores for me the importance of Ellen White's comment that "so closely will the counterfeit resemble the true that it will be impossible to distinguish between them except by the Holy Scriptures" and her advice that "by their testimony every statement and every miracle must be tested."

In *The Thunder of Justice*, from which I quoted extensively in a previous chapter, Ted and Maureen Flynn have this to say:

> There are doctrines concerning Our Lady which are not explicitly taught in Scripture, but which have been handed down through Holy Tradition, as faithful expressions of the beliefs and practices of the Church founded by Jesus Christ. Often Catholics speak of Scripture and Tradition as the sources of revelation. But perhaps it would be more accurate to speak of Scripture in Tradition, since every authentic teaching—whether oral or written—which has been handed down from the Apostles through their successors is part of Holy Tradition, the heritage of our Lord Jesus Christ (79).

> These times can easily be recognized as the "Marian Times" prophesied long ago in the writings

of various saints, who saw that as God chose to send Jesus to us the first time through a virgin, Mary, so He will choose the same for His Second Coming. *This truth is not declared outright in Scripture, nor can it be deduced by logical necessity. It is rather a matter of private revelation and a developing understanding under the guidance of the Holy Spirit of Mary's role in salvation history* (ibid., 16, emphasis supplied).

I suspect that when the testing time comes, God's people will be challenged over the very principle itself of "the Bible and the Bible only as the foundation of all faith and practice." The pressure to abandon this principle in favor of miracles that the whole world can see will be intense. It will be absolutely essential that we have this principle firmly embedded in our minds. Those who do not will be in great danger of yielding to the pressure to conform.

Once we have established the principle of the Bible alone as the basis for our beliefs, then we will need a clear understanding of the basic teachings of the Bible. A mere doctrinal, theoretical understanding of Bible truth, in the absence of a character developed in harmony with that truth, will not be enough to preserve our loyalty to God in the final crisis. However, even with a strong character and a close relationship with Jesus, those who have an incorrect theoretical view of such teachings as the state of the dead, the Sabbath, and the second coming of Christ[7] will be in great danger of succumbing to Satan's deceptions. We must never make the theoretical and devotional ways of understanding the Bible a matter of either-or. If you are weak in your theoretical understanding of the Bible, I urge you to make it a top priority in your life to correct this problem. Every Adventist Book Center has

I need to do this. Know the scriptures on these subjects + salvation also.

152

many books that can help you do this. I especially recommend the new *Bible Amplifier* series from Pacific Press as an excellent tool to help you study and understand the Bible for yourself.

A terrible crisis is coming upon the world. I believe it could easily happen within the lifetime of many who are reading this book. Therefore, preparation is utterly essential. I urge you to ask Jesus to help you develop a character that will stand through the end time. And begin devoting part of your devotional time to learning the basic truths of the Adventist message. By doing these simple things, you will go a long way toward preparing yourself for the terrible crisis that is surely coming upon the whole world in the very near future.

---

1. I don't mean to suggest that God's people will hate their enemies. But Genesis 3:15 does say that enmity will exist between God's people and the world.
2. Marvin Moore, *Conquering the Dragon Within* (Boise, Idaho: Pacific Press Publishing Association, 1995).
3. Michael Barkun, *Disaster and the Millennium* (New Haven, Conn.: Yale University Press, 1974).
4. Whether these apparitions will continue to occur during the season of calamity is impossible to say ahead of time. But there has been enough such activity in the recent past to give the world a very believable explanation of what's happening when the disasters of the end time begin to happen.
5. Mary's People, August 27, 1995, p. 12.
6. Ibid.
7. The rapture theory—what I call the "dual second coming" theory—is a deception that may cause many otherwise very good and sincere people to lose their way in the end time.

CHAPTER FIFTEEN

FACING THE END TIME
Without Fear

My wife and I have two friends who have told us about their fear of the end time. Both of them are in their early forties. One, a man, told me that when he was in grade school, a talk by a week of prayer speaker on end-time events so frightened him that to this day he has a hard time thinking about the subject. The other friend, a woman, grew up in a very conservative Adventist home where the end time was a common topic. Even now, she literally goes into a panic—uncontrollable shaking—any time she hears a discussion of the end time.

Adventists place a great deal of emphasis on end-time events, and fear of the end time is an extremely common problem among us. In a recent survey, an Adventist college religion professor found that 50 percent of the students in his eschatology classes were so afraid of the coming time of trouble they would rather be dead than face it!

I do not wish to deny that the information I have shared

with you in this book can be very frightening. I have no doubt that some of those reading this book have felt this fear. Some may have put the book down without finishing it; others may have refused to even read it.

So the question arises, How should we deal with these things? How can we handle the fear?

Some people deal with the problem by refusing to talk about end-time events. This is understandable in the case of those who were traumatized by talk of end-time events as children. However, I do believe it is possible to face the end time without fear. That's what I'd like to discuss with you in this concluding chapter.

The house afire

Suppose I knew that sometime in the next year your house would burn to the ground in the middle of the night. I would have no idea of the exact day—only that it would happen within the next twelve months.

Would you want me to tell you?

I suspect that most readers of this book would say Yes. Frightening as the information would be, they'd rather know so they could be prepared. Not to know could cost them their lives!

I believe God is sensitive to our feelings. I don't think He finds any joy in provoking us to fear unnecessarily. However, it was He, not I, who told His prophet Daniel, about 2,500 years ago, that there is coming "a time of distress such as has not happened from the beginning of nations until then" (Daniel 12:1). And it was none other than Jesus Himself who repeated Daniel's words, adding that "if those days had not been cut short, no one would survive" (Matthew 24:22).

So I make no apologies for talking about that time of distress in this book.

THE COMING GREAT CALAMITY

Some people may be distressed that Ellen White spoke so much about the final crisis and with such explicit language. She went so far as to say that "it is often the case that trouble is greater in anticipation than in reality; but this is not true of the crisis before us. The most vivid presentation cannot reach the magnitude of the ordeal."[1] Was Ellen White trying to scare God's people with this statement? Of course not! If the coming time of trouble will be a great danger to us, I would expect God to continually reveal more about it, especially as it draws near.

God has never refused to warn the world, and especially His own people, of the frightening future. Indeed, it is those who ignore these warnings who are overwhelmed. We have at least two excellent biblical examples of this.

For hundreds of years God warned the Israelites of the consequences of rebellion. As far back as the time of the Exodus, Moses devoted most of Deuteronomy 28 to the curses that would fall upon them for persistent disobedience. It doesn't make pleasant reading.

God's warnings grew increasingly frequent and alarming as the Jewish nation fell further and further into apostasy. By the time of the last prophet, Jeremiah (who actually experienced the destruction of Jerusalem), the warnings had reached a fever pitch. Jeremiah delivered God's message faithfully, but he was repeatedly accused of undermining the government. On at least one occasion he was imprisoned, and twice his life was threatened (see chapters 37, 26, 38).

The people did not like the bad news!

However, Jeremiah was right, and the people should have listened to His warnings and prepared. Because they refused, they were overwhelmed by the disaster when it came.

Several months before His arrest, trial, and execution,

Jesus warned His disciples of what was coming. However, because of their fear, they chose to ignore the warning (see Matthew 16:21, 22). And when the inevitable finally happened, they were overwhelmed. Indeed, they almost lost their faith! (see Luke 24:19-21; John 20:24, 25).

Thus I believe it is extremely important that we today pay careful attention to the warnings God has given us about the end time. If these warnings frighten us, rather than ignoring the message, we should deal with the fear.

The question is, how do we do that?

Jesus' advice for dealing with fear

Jesus taught an excellent lesson on how to deal with fear of trouble. Late one night He and His disciples were out on Lake Galilee when "without warning, a furious storm came up on the lake, so that the waves swept over the boat."

The disciples hit the panic button. "Lord," they cried, "save us! We're going to drown!"

Jesus, who had been sleeping in the back of the boat, roused Himself and said to His disciples, "You of little faith, why are you so afraid?" Then turning his face to the storm, "he rebuked the winds and the waves, and it was completely calm" (Matthew 8:23-26).

Jesus' answer to the disciples' fear was *faith!*

Please notice that He did not say, "Wow, that was a scary one!" He did not say, "Wasn't it awful of God to allow that storm to overwhelm us?" He did not say, "We got out of that one by the skin of our teeth!" He said, simply, "Where was your faith?"

Each of the other responses would have justified and encouraged the disciples' fears. But Jesus challenged them to trust God in the face of fear.

We must recognize, of course, that fear is a very normal human response to danger. We don't have to learn it. It's built in. We are born preprogrammed to respond with fear to dangerous situations.

If that is true, then why did Jesus reprove His disciples for their fear of the storm? Because their fear had turned into panic. It would have been perfectly appropriate for them to respond to their fear of the storm by baling water, steering the boat into the waves, and praying. It was not appropriate for them to lose their heads. It was not appropriate for them to allow their fear to take charge of their reason and control it.

The proper response to the storm, Jesus said, was faith—trusting God in the most traumatic emergency.

But that's a tall order! It doesn't come easily. How can we learn to keep our heads in the face of frightening situations?

Certainly a strong, consistent devotional life is the starting point. So much has been written about this that I hardly think I can add to it here, except for one thing: We need a strong devotional life *in the midst of trouble*.

Practicing with fear

Anything we humans learn to do well takes practice. We have to do the same thing over and over until we have learned to do it without making mistakes.

However, it is usually the case that we need an object or an instrument to practice *on*. For example: In order to play beautiful music on the piano, we must first have access to a piano. Then we must run our fingers over the keys many times for each piece we are learning until we can play it without making mistakes. In order to bake a good cake, we must have access to a variety of kitchen utensils and appliances. Then we must use those appliances many times until we can produce a perfect cake. In order to paint a straight line, we must have access to paint and a brush. By practicing with many crooked lines, we will eventually paint a straight one.

It's the same in spiritual life. God does not just hand us the ability to be fearless in the face of storms. We must practice it.

"Fine," you say, "but there aren't any tools for that like there are for learning how to play the piano, bake a cake, and paint a straight line." How can we practice having faith when there are no tools to practice it on?

Oh, but there are tools for practicing faith! We call them the *little* trials of life. By using each trial as an opportunity to practice our faith in God, we will eventually come to the place that we can trust Him completely in the face of the greatest storm.

Several years ago, when I was going through a particularly difficult trial, a friend said to me, "Marvin, a trial is a dangerous opportunity."

I like that!

The opportunity is the chance to strengthen our faith. The danger is that we may misuse the trial and actually weaken our faith.

There are many ways to misuse a trial. One way is to blame God for the trial: "Why did You let this happen to me?" Another is to blame ourselves: "I was so stupid to get myself into this mess!" Another way is to blame our trials on others: "Why is everyone against me?" Yet another way is self-pity: "Poor me!" Some people get very angry when trials come their way: "I'm going to roll some heads around here!" Others cut and run, like the disciples when Jesus was arrested in Gethsemane.

The faith answer to trials is to trust God. Trust in God keeps us calm in the storm. It keeps our emotions, especially fear, under the control of reason. Peter said, "In this [Christ's resurrection] you greatly rejoice, though now for a little while you may have had to suffer grief in all kinds of trials. *These have come so that your faith . . . may be proved genuine*" (1 Peter 1:6, 7, emphasis supplied).

But the faith answer to trials takes practice. It does not come naturally.

Keep in mind that with every trial we experience, you and I *will* practice. If we get angry, blame others, or pity ourselves, we are practicing that response to the next trial. If we lose our heads, we are developing that response. Some people get very "good" at these bad responses. When these responses have become habitual, we have developed a character defect.

If, on the other hand, we learn to trust God in each trial, we will have developed a character strength. Then, when the final crisis confronts us, we will be ready for it. Keep in mind that Ellen White began her statement about the final crisis in *Christ's Object Lessons* with the words, "It is in a crisis that character is revealed." Some of the virgins were prepared for the emergency, she said, and others were not. Then she said, "So now, a sudden, unlooked-for calamity, something that brings the soul face to face with death, *will show whether there is any real faith in the promises of God*" (412, emphasis supplied).

The primary issue in the final crisis will be our ability to trust in God. We cannot develop that ability to its fullest in an instant at the time the crisis comes. That's why the foolish virgins were—and will be—unprepared.

I am sure there will be varying degrees of preparation. Some will have a strong preparation, while others will have an adequate but minimum preparation. However, nobody will make it through the final crisis who has made no preparation whatsoever.

This means that today, tomorrow, and the next day, whatever the crises may be that come our way, we must determine not to blame God, ourselves, or anyone else, but to use them as tools to produce the faith we will need when the worst time of distress the world has ever known breaks upon us with blinding force. *Key*

Talking to children about the final crisis

I can still remember the day I first heard about the time of trouble. I was probably six or seven years old, and my mother read about it to my sister and me from *The Great Controversy*.

I cried.

My mother comforted me with the assurance that Jesus will protect His people, and I'm sure that helped. But I can still remember feeling very afraid.

One of the major challenges facing Adventist parents in this age of earth's history is when and how to tell their children about the coming time of trouble. It is also a challenge that confronts pastors, teachers, and anyone else who may talk to children about the end time. The stories of my two friends that I used to introduce this chapter illustrate well the importance of being careful how we talk to children about the end time.

Because I have made a major study of the end time during the past few years, I have had a number of people ask me how they can tell their children about the time of trouble in a way that will not cause them to feel afraid. And my answer is very simple: I don't think it's possible to do that.

God created the human mind to feel fear of danger. If you were out in the jungle on a dark night and you heard a loud roar fifty feet off to one side of the trail, you would feel fear. You could not stop the fear, and you would not want to. The fear would motivate you to protect yourself by running. That's why God built the capacity to experience fear into our psyches, and it's why He made it instinctive—an automatic response that doesn't take thinking on our part.

Even in the end time, I believe that we should do everything within reason to protect ourselves when we are threatened. Jesus advised His disciples, "When you are persecuted in one place, flee to another" (Matthew 10:23). That's using normal fear in a proper way.

However, there is a difference between normal fear and panic. Normal fear is under the control of reason. But when we panic, reason goes by the way, and our behavior is totally under the control of our fear.

There is a certain amount of normal fear associated with our anticipation of the time of trouble, and we should not deny this when we talk to our children about it. In fact, one of the best things we can do is to allow our children to express their very normal fear and then lead them to trust in Jesus. Trust will not and should not remove their normal fear, but it will help them to keep that fear under the control of reason.

At what age should we talk to children about these things? I believe we should talk to very young children about the joys of the second coming of Jesus rather than about the time of trouble. When we do begin talking to them about the coming crisis, we should keep our remarks brief and simple, without much detail. By age six most children can probably handle this kind of explanation. Increasingly, as they get older, we can explain more, so that by the time they are junior-age they have a fairly clear idea of what lies ahead.

Some parents may think this is too much too soon. I would point out, however, that if your children do not learn these things from you, they will almost certainly hear about them from someone else who may not be as wise as you in their explanation. If you want to ensure that your children hear about the trauma of the end time for the first time from you, then you should tell them yourself before they are likely to hear about it from others.

I believe that junior-age children are capable of handling this information if it is presented to them properly. Several years ago I had the privilege of speaking on the end time for several days at the Mountain View camp meeting in West Virginia. Partway through the series, the leader of the junior department asked if I would speak about the end time to his children. With some trepidation, I agreed to do so. But I was amazed. After I had made a rather simple presentation about earth's final events, those juniors peppered me with the same questions that adults ask. The issues they raised were profound. And they would not stop! It went on for an hour, and the children still wanted to know more. I finally had to bring the meeting to a close myself!

One of the questions the children asked was how to anticipate the end time without being afraid. And I told them frankly that there is no way to do that. But then I explained that we must learn to trust Jesus, who will be our guardian during the end time.

The following letter to the editor appeared in the *Adventist Review* a number of years ago in response to a special issue on the second coming of Christ:

> I have spent years trying to neutralize fears and horrors that have become associated with the Second Coming. Even today adults from my parents' generation often speak with doom and dread when discussing President Bush's conservatism or changing

events in the former Soviet Union. If Christ's coming is an exciting event, why is the focus so consistently upon the horrifying events of "the time of trouble"? This served only to make me dread the last days, and feel guilty doing so.

As a mother of two small children, I have made it a goal to share only the exciting, incredibly wonderful aspects of Jesus, heaven, and His second coming. Worry and anxiety will come naturally as a part of growing up in a world with many problems. My second goal is to impart a sense of trust in our heavenly Father. My children need to know He keeps us safe and guides us, and that one day at a time is all we should concern ourselves with.

I have to ask myself, How and what would Jesus teach our children about His coming? Would He focus on persecution, death, and horrible things, or would He want them to know the joys of His coming will mean to them personally? I choose the latter. I want this event to evoke only feelings of anticipation and visions of happiness, not of dread and insecurity. I want my children to grow into adults who can cherish the thought of His return, not shrink from it.[2]

I like that. It sounds to me as though this mother's children were probably preschoolers at the time she wrote this letter. That is precisely the age when she needs to be talking about the joys of Jesus' coming, heaven, and eternal life, and not the time of trouble that will precede them. I also like her focus on teaching her children to trust Jesus, who "keeps us safe and guides us." I like her comment that "one day at a time is all we should concern ourselves with."

My only caution to this mother (and others like her) would be that she should not assume she can shield her children forever from a knowledge of the time of trouble, nor should she want to. God revealed to us something of what that time will be like because He wanted us to know so that we can be prepared. Adult Christians need a mature understanding of that time and how to cope with it through trust in Jesus, but they can't develop this trust if they are forever prevented from knowing about it lest they feel afraid.

Even those who are not parents need to be cautious. For example, if you are among those Adventist adults who enjoy meeting together on Friday evenings and Sabbath afternoons (or at any other time, for that matter) for long theological discussions, you need to be careful what you say about the end time when children are present. If preschoolers are within earshot, you should avoid saying anything about the time of trouble. Around older children, gauge your conversation to their age, and always emphasize trust in God.

Looking at the other side

I heard the story once of a woman who did lots of embroidery. One day a friend came to visit and started complaining about all the trials she was suffering. The woman showed her friend the backside of the piece she was embroidering at the moment and asked her if she didn't think it was a beautiful piece of work. Her friend said, "No, it's horrible!" The woman then turned the cloth over and showed her friend the front side. It truly *was* beautiful.

It's easy, in this life, to view the time of trouble from the backside. God has purposely shown it to us because we need to know about it. I'm glad, though, that He has also given us glimpses of the front side. I would like to conclude this chapter—and this book—with a beautiful picture from Revelation that shows God's people in heaven *after* the time of trouble:

> And I saw what looked like a sea of glass mixed with fire and, standing beside the sea, those who had been victorious over the beast and his image and over the number of his name. They held harps given them by God and sang the song of Moses the servant of God and the song of the Lamb:
> "Great and marvelous are your deeds,
> Lord God Almighty.
> Just and true are your ways,
> King of the ages.
> Who will not fear you, O Lord,
> and bring glory to your name?
> For you alone are holy.
> All nations will come and worship before you,
> for your righteous acts have been revealed
> (Revelation 15:2-4).

This word picture gives us a faint glimpse of the unspeakable joys of heaven. But notice that those who praise God so joyfully are able to do so because they had been "victorious over the beast and his image and over the number of his name." Those who sing this song in heaven someday will be those who have learned on this earth to trust Jesus during the most traumatic trial that Christians have ever had to face. That's why they will be able to sing with such exuberance then.

I want to be a part of that group. Don't you?

---

1. *The Great Controversy*, 622.
2. *Adventist Review*, 27 February 1992, 2.

APPENDIX A

REFLECTIONS
on the
Close of Probation

In this appendix I would like to introduce you to some thoughts about the close of probation that may be new to you. Much of what I share with you will be stated quite explicitly by the inspired evidence, but in some cases my conclusions will be an interpretation of the evidence.

I will be using the expression *close of probation* in a variety of ways in this appendix, and this could easily lead to confusion. To avoid that, I need to define exactly what I mean by each of the ways I will use the term.

Adventists have traditionally understood the close of probation to be that moment when Jesus ceases His mediatorial ministry in the heavenly sanctuary, after which every human being's destiny will be fixed for eternity. From that point on in world history, no one can be saved who has not already accepted Jesus as his or her Saviour. From now on, when I refer to the close of probation in this final sense, I will call it "the final close of human probation." The following chart, which is probably quite familiar to you, illustrates this way of thinking about the close of probation:

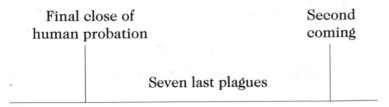

Final close of
human probation

Second
coming

Seven last plagues

While this is what Adventists most often mean when they talk about the *close of probation*, it is not the only way we use the term. In a sense, this appendix and the next one are simply a definition of some of these other ways of using the expression "close of probation."

Individual and Corporate Close of Probation

I find it helpful to distinguish between individual and group probation. In the following statement Ellen White refers to both:

> Through a certain period of probation He [God] exercises longsuffering toward nations, cities, and individuals (*Review and Herald*, 2 May 1893).

If God grants "a certain period of probation" to both individuals and groups (nations and cities), it is logical to conclude that the probation of both individuals and groups can close. Let's examine the close of both individual and group probation more closely, beginning with individual close of probation.

Individual close of probation

All human probation does not close each time an individual closes his or her probation. Thus the close of an individual's probation is quite a different thing from the final close of all human probation.

Individuals can close their probation in either of two ways. At the present time, the most common way is for a person to die. However, some people also close their probation when they make a final and irrevocable decision for or against Jesus Christ and eternal salvation. When a living individual's probation closes on God's side, his holy character is sealed and God guarantees him eternal life in His kingdom. When an individual's probation closes on Satan's side, his evil character is sealed, and he is guaranteed to suffer eternal death. (We call this the sin against the Holy Spirit.) That is what the words in Revelation 22:11 mean: "He that is unjust, let him be unjust still; . . . and he that is righteous, let him be righteous still" (KJV).

During the time that a person's probation is open, he or she is free to switch from God's side to Satan's side and vice versa. However, once an individual's probation has closed on one side, that person can never switch to the other side.

Group close of probation

Ellen White said that God also grants probationary time to nations and cities. Thus, groups of people can also close their probation. From now on, when I speak of a group closing its probation, I will call it "corporate close of probation." A group's corporate probation can close in one of two ways. First, when the individual probation of each member of a group closes, that group's corporate probation may close. The other way is for a group's corporate probation to close even though the probation of most

The organizations or nation probation is over

members within the group remains open. This distinction is so important to our discussion in this appendix and the next one that I would like to repeat it for you:

• Corporate close of probation may occur when all members of a group have closed their individual probation.

• Corporate close of probation may occur even though the probation of most members of the group remains open.

I would like to call your attention to several examples of each of these. We will begin with examples of situations when corporate probation closed for a group as a whole because the probation of each member of the group had closed.

When all individual probations have closed. Without a doubt, the most outstanding example of this is Noah's flood. Those who refused to enter the ark following Noah's final appeal closed their individual probations. The corporate probation of the entire world closed when an angel shut the door of the ark.[1] Then the flood came. The same thing happened at the destruction of Sodom and Gomorrah. When every individual in those cities with the exception of Lot and his wife and two daughters had closed their individual probations, the corporate probation of the two cities closed, and then the fire fell.

Ellen White gives us one more example of a corporate close of probation in which the probation of every individual in the group had also closed—the Amorite nation. She says:

> [God] allows to nations a certain period of probation, and gives them evidences of His requirements . . . [But] when iniquity is full, as in the case of the Amorites, God takes the matter in

hand, and His judgments are not longer withheld (*The Youth's Instructor*, 1 February 1894).

This form of corporate close of probation—when each individual has closed his or her probation—is also what will exist at the final close of probation just before the outpouring of the seven last plagues.

Corporate probation closes, individual probations do not. It is also possible for a group's corporate probation to close while the probations of individuals within that group remain largely open. Probably the best example of this is the close of probation for the Jewish nation. When the Jewish leaders rejected Stephen's appeal before the Sanhedrin, the Jews closed their national probation. From that time forward, they ceased to be God's chosen people. *Yet individual Jews could still be saved*.

This concept of corporate close of probation, such as for a nation, while the probation of individuals within that nation remains open, will be very important to our discussion later in this appendix.

Ellen White informs us of at least one instance in the future when a nation will close its probation as a nation even though the individual probations of most of its citizens will remain open. Regarding the United States of America, she says:

> As the approach of the Roman armies was a sign to the disciples of the impending destruction of Jerusalem, so may this apostasy [a national Sunday law] be a sign to us that the limit of God's forbearance is reached, that the measure of our nation's iniquity is full, and that the angel of mercy is about to take her flight, never to return (*Testimonies for the Church*, 5:451).

THE COMING GREAT CALAMITY

The words *the measure of iniquity is full*, in the usual Adventist understanding of the expression, mean that the individual or group to which the words are applied have reached the point that their probation is about to be closed. This is confirmed by Ellen White's next words: "The angel of mercy is about to take her flight, never to return." Yet Adventists for the past one hundred fifty years have understood that at the point of this national Sunday law the final warning will have just begun. Many people will join with us after that. Obviously, the probation of the American people as a whole will remain open beyond the point that the nation's corporate probation has closed.

Judgments Follow the Close of Probation

One of the most significant implications of a corporate close of probation is that it opens the way for God's judgments to fall. We see biblical examples of this in the destruction of cities (Sodom and Gomorrah), nations (the Amorites and the Jews), and the entire world (the Flood). In each case, judgments followed immediately after the group's corporate close of probation.

In the case of the antediluvians, the inhabitants of Sodom and Gomorrah, and the Amorites, the judgments of God destroyed the people themselves, because the entire population had closed their individual probations. The Jews, on the other hand, continued to exist as a race, because the people as a whole had not closed their individual probations. Thus only their national government was destroyed.

Ellen White suggests that judgments from God will also follow America's corporate close of probation in the future, even though the nation's government will probably continue to function:[2]

When the state shall use its power to enforce the decrees and sustain the institutions of the church—then will Protestant America have formed an image to the papacy, and there will be a national apostasy which will only end in national ruin (*Seventh-day Adventist Bible Commentary*, 7:976).

The story of the destruction of Sodom and Gomorrah provides us with an interesting insight into how God calculates when to bring His judgments. You will recall that Abraham, pleading for the cities of the plain, asked whether God would bring His fiery judgments if fifty faithful souls could be found in the cities. God said No. Abraham then reduced the number to forty-five, then to forty, thirty, twenty, and ten. Even if ten faithful souls could be found, God said He would not destroy the cities. Unfortunately, only four could be found, *and these God rescued from the devastation before it occurred*. We find the same pattern with the Flood. Only eight people were found faithful, and God saved them out of the Flood in the ark.

From this we learn that God is extremely patient with sinful human beings. He will not cut off our corporate probation, whatever group we may belong to, until rebellion is well-nigh universal. And I believe He is just as patient with individuals. That's the good news about the close of probation!

The Close of the World's Probation as a World

Now let's apply what we have discussed thus far in this chapter to the future of the world as a whole. I believe that a time is coming when the world will close its corporate probation as a world in the same way that the Jewish nation closed its probation as a nation. This will open the way for

world will close its probation, even though some
people in the world can + will still decide on
THE COMING GREAT CALAMITY
which side they will trust

the most terrible natural disasters—warning judgments from God—to fall upon the earth. These disasters will not mark the final close of all human probation though. Rather, they will set in motion the final warning. The close of probation for individuals will by and large remain open for a period of time, giving them a chance to respond to the final warning. We have seen the following diagram several times in this book. Now it is time to add one other element to it:

Close of the world's probation as a world	Final close of human probation	Second coming
warning	*you & me* *punishment*	

THE FINAL CRISIS

here   I believe that when the final crisis breaks upon the world, the world's probation as a world will have closed. This will open the way for the terrible judgments of God we have been talking about to fall, which will warn the world that the final close of human probation is approaching.

The Close of Probation and the Delay

When Jesus gave His famous sermon on signs of the end (see Matthew 24, Mark 13, and Luke 21), He combined His description of the destruction of Jerusalem with His description of the end of the world. In doing this, He made the destruction of Jerusalem and the events leading up to it a type of the end of the world. Most Adventists agree that this is a valid principle for interpreting Jesus' prophecy,[3] so let's compare the destruction of Jerusalem (the type) with the end of the world (the antitype). I will especially call attention to the delay in the implementation of the destruction of Jerusalem and its implications for our own time.

I think it is safe to assume that when the Jews closed their probation as a nation, God's judgments *could* have followed immediately—even as soon as the next day, and certainly within a few months. However, God chose to delay those judgments for nearly forty years, and for a very good reason. Had He executed His judgments against Jerusalem and Judea immediately, He would have destroyed the seedbed His infant church needed in which to mature. But as soon as the gospel had put down its roots deep enough in Asia Minor[4] and Europe that His church could survive the destruction of its birthplace, God's destructive judgments fell on the Jewish nation.

Since the destruction of Jerusalem and the events leading up to it are a type of the second coming of Christ and the events leading up to it, can we expect that God will also delay the implementation of His destructive judgments in our day? Revelation 7:1-4 suggests that this will indeed be the case: *read openly*

> After this I saw four angels standing at the four corners of the earth, holding back the four winds of the earth to prevent any wind from blowing on the land or on the sea or on any tree. Then I saw another angel coming up from the east, having the seal of the living God. He called out in a loud voice to the four angels who had been given power to harm the land and the sea: "Do not harm the land or the sea or the trees until we put a seal on the foreheads of the servants of our God." Then I heard the number of those who were sealed: 144,000 from all the tribes of Israel.

Notice that the time for God's destructive judgments to fall on the earth to harm the land, the sea, and the trees has clearly come. I believe this means that the world's corporate probation has closed, and the way has been opened for God's destructive judgments to fall. However, an angel from heaven rushes to the earth and calls for a delay in the implementation of that plan. This sounds very much like the delay that occurred in God's implementation of destructive judgments against the Jewish nation. And, just as there was a reason for the delay in the destruction of the Jewish nation, so there will be a reason for the delay in God's destructive judgments at the end of the world: The 144,000 need time to be sealed.

Traditionally Adventists have taught that the four winds will be released at the final close of human probation, and we have identified the blowing of the winds (the harming of the land, sea, and trees) with the seven last plagues after the close of probation. Here is how this view of the four winds looks on a chart. Pay special attention to the elements in the chart that are shaded and notice where they are located in relation to the boldfaced and italicized items:

THE TRADITIONAL ADVENTIST VIEW
OF THE FOUR WINDS

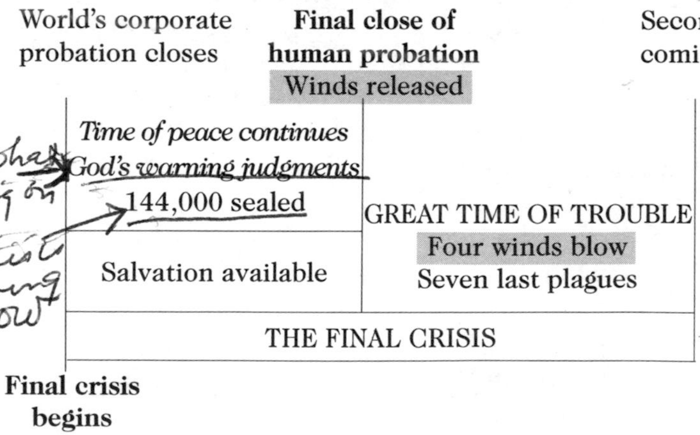

World's corporate probation closes	**Final close of human probation** Winds released	Second coming
Time of peace continues *God's warning judgments* 144,000 sealed	GREAT TIME OF TROUBLE	
Salvation available	Four winds blow Seven last plagues	
THE FINAL CRISIS		

Final crisis begins

[handwritten note in left margin: that's what is going on now. Then this is also going on, wow]

MARVIN MOORE

Please notice that on this diagram the four winds are released at the final close of human probation. This way of outlining these events presents us with a problem though. The judgments of God before the final close of human probation that Ellen White describes are extremely severe, making it difficult to think of that period as the time of peace and calm that the angel from heaven called for during the delay. Thus, I would like you to consider the possibility that the four angels will release the four winds a short time before the final close of probation, and the delay must occur prior to that. This idea is a bit complex, so you may wish to spend a few moments examining the following chart. Compare the shaded elements in this chart with those same elements in the previous chart. Note especially their relationship to the final close of human probation and the beginning of the final crisis, which are in boldfaced type on each chart:

REVISED VIEW OF
THE FOUR WINDS

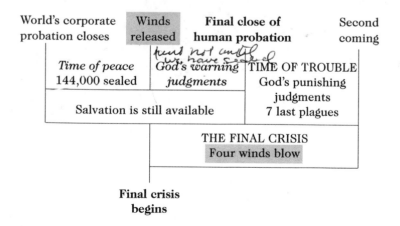

World's corporate probation closes	**Winds released**	**Final close of human probation**	Second coming
Time of peace 144,000 sealed	*God's warning judgments*	TIME OF TROUBLE God's punishing judgments 7 last plagues	
Salvation is still available			
	THE FINAL CRISIS Four winds blow		

**Final crisis
begins**

THE COMING GREAT CALAMITY

According to this diagram, the blowing of the four winds refers to God's destructive judgments during the entire period of the final crisis, both before and after the final close of human probation.

I want to conclude this discussion about the close of probation by saying that the ideas expressed are for your thoughtful consideration, not for debate or argumentation. They are tentative—a suggestion. This is especially true of the chart at the bottom of page 177.

---

1. Some people probably made the final decision that closed their individual probation long before the door of the ark was shut.
2. Bible prophecy suggests that the second beast of Revelation 13, which Adventists have historically considered to be the United States government, will not be destroyed until the second coming of Christ (see Revelation 19:19, 20; a comparison of verse 20 with chapter 13:13 shows that the false prophet is the same as the second beast of Revelation 13).
3. For those who like inspired evidence for such conclusions, here it is: "The scenes that transpired at the destruction of Jerusalem will be repeated at the great and terrible day of the Lord, but in a more fearful manner" (*Selected Messages*, 3:417).
4. The biblical Asia Minor corresponds roughly to the borders of modern Turkey.

QUESTIONS ABOUT

Christ's Object Lessons, 412

In this appendix, I will comment on two questions I have been asked in regard to Ellen White's statement on page 412 of *Christ's Object Lessons* about a "sudden, unlooked-for calamity." This statement is the basis for the title of this book—*The Coming Great Calamity*, and one of the questions has a direct bearing on the meaning of that title. I quoted this statement in chapter 3, "The Coming Judgments of God," but we need to read it again before beginning this discussion:

It is in a crisis that character is revealed. When the earnest voice proclaimed at midnight, "Behold, the bridegroom cometh; go ye out to meet him," and the sleeping virgins were roused from their slumbers, it was seen who had made preparation for the event. Both parties were taken unawares; but one was prepared for the emergency, and the other was found without preparation. So now, a sudden and unlooked-for calamity, something that brings the soul face to face with death, will show whether there is any real faith in the promises of God. It will show whether the soul is sustained by grace. The great final test comes at the close of human probation, when it will be too late for the soul's need to be supplied (*Christ's Object Lessons*, 412).

I will discuss two questions that arise out of this statement. First, when she spoke of "a sudden, unlooked-for calamity," was Ellen White predicting a future calamity that will be experienced by the entire church at the time of the final crisis, or did she have in mind the individual calamities that can come to any of us at any time? And second, if she had in mind a future calamity that will be experienced by the entire Christian church, what is the relationship of this calamity to the close of probation?

The calamity and the final crisis

I have taken the position in this book that the "sudden, unlooked-for calamity" refers to a specific natural disaster that will alert all God's people around the world at the same time that Christ's second coming is near. However, several people have questioned this, some quite strongly. They understand Ellen White to mean not a specific calamity in the future, but any calamity that may happen in the life of any Christian at any time. The following diagram outlines the issues succinctly:

Position A: Ellen White had in mind Christians
  • Individually
  • At any time

Position B: Ellen White had in mind Christians
- Corporately—the entire church
- Eschatologically—at the end of time

My view is obviously the second one. Part of my reason for this interpretation is the fact that Ellen White uses the singular—"*a calamity*." While she speaks of multiple calamities during the final crisis in other places, I have assumed that here she refers to the first of these many calamities. Thus my title: *The Coming Great Calamity*.

However, if, in writing these words, Ellen White had in mind any calamity that can strike any Christian at any time, then my title is quite unjustified. It is valid only if she intended us to understand a calamity that will be experienced by the entire Christian church at the end of time.

Those who take the position that she is speaking of individual Christians at any time refer to the following statement from *Review and Herald*, 17 September 1895. Notice that it is quite similar to the one in *Christ's Object Lessons:*

Character is revealed in a crisis. When the earnest voice proclaimed at midnight, "Behold, the bridegroom cometh; go ye out to meet him," the sleeping virgins roused from their slumbers, and it was seen who had made preparation for the event. Both parties were taken unawares, but one was prepared for the emergency, and the other was found without preparation. Character is revealed by circumstances. Emergencies bring out the true metal of character. Some sudden and unlooked-for calamity, bereavement, or crisis, some unexpected sickness or anguish, something that brings the soul face to face with death, will bring out the true inwardness of the character. It will be made manifest whether or not there is any real faith in the promises of the word of God. It will be made manifest whether or not the soul is sustained by grace, whether there is oil in the vessel with the lamp.

It is very evident that in this statement Ellen White is speaking about *individual* calamities that may happen to any of us *at any time*. She speaks of "bereavement, or crisis, some unexpected sickness or anguish." Thus I concur fully with those who affirm that in this statement Ellen White has in mind a broad spectrum of individual calamities that can happen at any time, and not a single, worldwide calamity that introduces the final crisis. The question is this: Does she mean the same thing when she speaks of "a sudden, unlooked-for calamity" in *Christ's Object Lessons?*

The similarity between the two statements makes it quite obvious that she lifted the statement out of the *Review and Herald* article and dropped it, slightly modified, into her chapter in *Christ's Object Lessons*. Thus, as we begin our examination of the statement in the book, it is reasonable to assume, at least tentatively, that she means the same thing as in the article. However, we must also grant her the freedom to express a thought in the statement as it appears in the book that is different from the thought she intended in the article, particularly since she changed the wording in the book.

And, indeed, there is good reason to believe that in *Christ's Object Lessons* she has in mind the *corporate* experience of the Christian church in an *eschatological* setting, not *individual* calamities *at any time*.

To begin with, Ellen White did not just lift the entire article from the *Review and Herald* and drop it with slight modifications into her book. The two paragraphs we have been considering are the only ones between the *Review and Herald* article and the chapter in *Christ's Object Lessons* that are anywhere near the same. And when we compare the two documents, we discover that the chapter in *Christ's Object Lessons* applies the parable in a significantly different manner from the *Review and Herald* article. The article applies the parable more to the individual at any time in history. The book views the parable much more from a corporate and eschatological perspective.

Let's examine Ellen White's handling of the parable in the book first, and then we will discuss how she treats the parable in the article.

The corporate, eschatological interpretation of the parable in *Christ's Object Lessons* is evident almost from the beginning of the chapter. On the second page of this chapter, Ellen White said that when Christ told His disciples the story of the ten virgins, He was "*illustrating the experience of the church that shall live just before His second coming*" (406). Two things are important about this sentence. First, Ellen White indicates that she is going to examine the parable of the ten virgins as it applies to the experience of the entire Christian church, not the experience of individual Christians; and second, she is going to examine the parable from the perspective of the church that exists in the world "just before His second coming." In other words, she is going to apply the parable *corporately* and *eschatologically*, not *individually* and *at any time*.

We find the same thought expressed on page 408:

> In the parable, all the ten virgins went out to meet the bridegroom. All had lamps and vessels

for oil. For a time there was seen no difference between them. *So with the church that lives just before Christ's second coming.*

Again, Ellen White applied the parable to the experience of the entire Christian church at the end of time— *corporately* and *eschatologically*, not *individually* and *at any time*.

This is the context that precedes the "sudden, unlooked-for calamity" statement in *Christ's Object Lessons.* Let's take a moment to examine the context that follows, beginning with the paragraph that comes immediately after:

> The ten virgins are watching in the evening of this earth's history. All claim to be Christians. All have a call, a name, a lamp, and all profess to be doing God's service. All apparently wait for Christ's appearing. But five are unready. Five will be found surprised, dismayed, outside the banquet hall.

Notice again Ellen White's end-time application of the parable: The ten virgins are watching "*in the evening of this earth's history.*" And notice the corporate application: *All* [the virgins] claim to be Christians. *All* have a call, a name, a lamp," etc. Throughout the remainder of the chapter Ellen White continues this end-time, corporate application of the parable. A couple of examples will suffice, lest I weary you:

> The coming of the bridegroom was at midnight—the darkest hour. <u>So the coming of Christ will take place in the darkest period of this earth's history</u> (414).

[handwritten note:] I thought the darkest hour is just before dawn 184? ~ same meaning—

This statement is clearly eschatological—something that is totally absent in the 17 September 1895 *Review and Herald* article. The following statement is both eschatological and corporate:

> Thus in the night of spiritual darkness God's glory is to shine forth through His church in lifting up the bowed down and comforting those that mourn (417).

In a different setting, the "night of spiritual darkness" that Ellen White speaks of here could refer to more than one period of earth's history. However, in the context of the chapter as a whole, it clearly applies to the darkest period of earth's history—the weeks and months immediately preceding the second coming of Christ. And it is the *church*—the corporate body of Christian believers—that is to minister to the world at that time.

This is how Ellen White treats the parable of the ten virgins in *Christ's Object Lessons*. What is her approach in the *Review and Herald?*

Like the chapter in the book, the entire article is an interpretation of the parable of the ten virgins. However, from beginning to end, the article is spiritual advice about surrender and character transformation that is appropriate for individual Christians at any time. Nowhere does Ellen White apply the parable to the corporate church in the last days.

The article does use plural pronouns a great deal—we, us, they, them, etc. But the advice seems especially relevant to individual Christian experience. A couple of examples will suffice:

> They [Christians like the wise virgins] understand that the Christian's character should

represent the character of Christ, and be full of grace and truth. To them is imparted the oil of grace, which sustains a never-failing light.

Testing times come to all. How do we conduct ourselves under the test and proving of God? Do our lamps go out? or do we still keep them burning? Are we prepared for every emergency by our connection with Him who is full of grace and truth?

There is no effort here to apply the parable eschatologically or to the church as a whole. While the pronouns are plural, Ellen White's advice is quite individual. I find it especially significant that the second statement refers to a "testing time," but it is applicable to all Christians at any time in history. She makes no effort to apply the parable to the final eschatological test.

Another point to consider is that the word *church* appears only once in the entire *Review and Herald* article, and nothing in the way it is used suggests that the parable as a whole be understood corporately. She says:

They [the foolish virgins] are attached to those who believe the truth, and go with them, having lamps, which represent a knowledge of the truth. When there was a revival in the *church*, their feelings were stirred; but they failed to have oil in their vessels, because they did not bring the principles of godliness into their daily life and character (emphasis supplied).

Clearly, in this reference to the church, Ellen White is not giving us a metaphor for the interpretation of the parable as a whole. Also, notice again that though Ellen White uses plural pronouns, the application she makes is especially relevant to personal Christian experience. This is pervasive throughout the article.

Now that we have examined the article in the *Review and Herald* and the chapter in *Christ's Object Lessons* as a whole, we need to compare the two "calamity" paragraphs themselves. In both cases, Ellen White begins the paragraph by calling attention to the fact that character is revealed in a crisis. Then she tells us what the crisis was in the lives of the ten virgins at Christ's time: The midnight cry that the bridegroom was on the way. Here is how she says it in *Christ's Object Lessons* (the wording is almost identical in the *Review and Herald*):

> When the earnest voice proclaimed at midnight, "Behold, the bridegroom cometh; go ye out to meet him," and the sleeping virgins were roused from their slumbers, it was seen who had made preparation for the event. Both parties were taken unawares; but one was prepared for the emergency, and the other was found without preparation.

The entire focus of these sentences is on the midnight cry and the crisis that this event precipitated in the lives of the ten women.

Now notice the very next words in *Christ's Object Lessons*: "So now . . . ." Ellen White is going to apply the crisis moment in the lives of the ten virgins to some crisis moment in the lives of God's people today.

And what is that crisis?

In the *Review and Herald* article, it is "some . . . bereavement, or crisis, some unexpected sickness or anguish"—most any crisis in the daily life of any Christian at any time in history. But in *Christ's Object Lessons* the crisis moment is "the great final test" that occurs "at the close of human probation."

The "great final test" that Ellen White speaks about here cannot be just any crisis in the life of any Christian. She is referring to a very specific moment in the history of God's church on earth: The final crisis "at the close of human probation" that will be experienced at the same time by all His people everywhere. If you doubt that this crisis will be worldwide, read Revelation 13! And Ellen White says that *this* will be the moment of the midnight cry that awakens God's sleeping church.

However, the "great final test" is not what will awaken the virgins. They will be awakened by a "sudden, unlooked-for calamity," and I suggest that the same calamity that awakens them will also create the crisis that tests their characters.

Now let me ask you a question. What kind of a "sudden, unlooked-for calamity" will it take to awaken God's sleeping saints all over the world at one time and thrust them into earth's "great final test"? Certainly none of the natural disasters that have occurred on earth since the Flood have done that. I suggest that a calamity powerful enough to awaken God's people all over the world at one time and thrust them into "the great final test" will have to be of the magnitude that we discussed earlier in this book—so terrible that it will threaten the survival of the entire human race. Nothing else could create such a crisis.

It is true that many such calamities will occur at that time. Ellen White says these calamities will be "most awful, most unexpected," and they will "follow one after another" (*Evangelism*, 27). I am also sure that each calamity will intensify the struggle between God's people and the world. However, just as a pregnant woman is awakened from her sleep by the first labor pain, not the last one, so surely the calamity that awakens God's worldwide church at the end of time will be the first one, not the last one. Logic demands that it be so!

One point I think we need to recognize is that the calamity could be something other than a natural disaster—war, perhaps, or a worldwide financial collapse. *to are here now* Certainly all these things will be part of the end-time scenario. My justification for suggesting that it is a natural disaster is the entire context of this book. Since Ellen White and the Bible make it clear that natural disasters will create a terrible crisis in the world, it seems reasonable to me to understand the "sudden, unlooked-for calamity" in *Christ's Object Lessons* that way as well.

I also think we need to consider the possibility that Ellen White's "sudden, unlooked-for calamity," while in the singular, could be understood to refer to all the calamities we've been talking about in this book—the entire period of the final crisis. However, as I pointed out a moment ago, if the "season of calamity" will include many calamities, then there will have to be a first one in the series.

That is why I have titled this book, *The Coming Great Calamity*.

Having said all this, however, I wish to add that I respect the view of those who disagree with me—who believe the calamity Ellen White speaks of on page 412 of *Christ's Object Lessons* is something other than a worldwide natural disaster that awakens all God's sleeping saints at the end of time. There has to be room for friendly differences of opinion among God's people. This issue is *not* worth quarreling about!

The great calamity will be a catalyst for the Sunday law

189

THE COMING GREAT CALAMITY

Relationship of the calamity to the close of probation

Ellen White's statement that "the great final test" will come "*at* the close of human probation" makes it appear that the "sudden, unlooked-for calamity" will occur at the same time as the close of probation. However, in this book I have taken the position that it will precede the close of probation by a short time. *we are here*

We must keep in mind that this great final test is what will divide the world into two camps so that probation can close. Thus the test cannot come *at* the close of probation in the most absolute sense. It must precede the close of probation by enough time that people are able to make up their minds one way or the other after it occurs. Thus Ellen White's statement that the test will come *at* the close of probation must be understood in a general sense.

If you read Appendix A, you know that I understand the close of probation in two ways: (1) as the point in time when Christ ceases His mediatorial ministry, and (2) as the short period of time just before that (the time of the judgment of the living), during which all human beings will be closing their individual probations. I believe it is this latter *period* of time that we must understand Ellen White to have in mind when she speaks of the close of probation in her "sudden, unlooked-for calamity" statement. If all this sounds a bit confusing to you, I recommend that you read Appendix A and then read again what I have said here.

---

* Ellen White often lifted statements from earlier writings and dropped them into later writings, sometimes word-for-word, other times slightly changed. In the case of these two statements, the one from *Review and Herald* is the earlier one since it was published in 1895, while *Christ's Object Lessons* was published in 1900.

Other Books by Marvin Moore

The Crisis of the End Time

A storm is coming. This is the big one. But despite the sound of distant thunder, most don't know what's coming.

With compelling evidence from Scripture and the Spirit of Prophecy, Marvin Moore suggests that the greatest crisis in human history is about to break upon us with startling speed and ferocity. He also shows how each of us can keep our relationship with Jesus during earth's darkest hour.

Not for a long time has there been such a forceful, yet easy-to-understand explanation of the vital issues our church and our world are about to face. *The Crisis of the End Time* will help you walk with Jesus today and through the coming storm without fear.

Pacific Press.
Paper, 256 pages.
US$10.99/Cdn$15.99.

Conquering the Dragon Within

This book is a pointed reminder to Christians living in the end time that the Dragonslayer lives! For those serious about preparing characters that will stand through the upcoming crisis, this book is a reminder that when Prince Michael moves into a human heart, the dragon retreats. Drawing on the counsel of the Bible, the Spirit of Prophecy, and the Twelve-Step recovery movement, author Marvin Moore shows us that through Christ, character change and victory over sin are possible, even certain. We can conquer the dragon within.

Pacific Press.
Hard back, 314 pages.
US$13.99/Cdn$20.49.

Order today! 1-800-765-6955

are you serving your Heavenly
Father or the earthly version of
your Heavenly Father.

The more you slow down
the more you can get
done. Merci

earthly version of my Heavenly Father:
— has favorites
— I will never be good enough,
  but others who don't even try
  just are
— doesn't know me or care to
  really know me
— is not compassionate to me, but
  has compassion for those who
  use her
— remarks that let me know I
  am judgemental because I
  don't think what happens w/the
  favorites is good
— I am selfish — I have only
  myself to take care of
— I don't deserve a home because
  I am alone
—